E242
EDUCATION: A SECOND-LEVEL COU

LEARNING FOR ALL

UNIT 1/2
MAKING CONNECTIONS

Prepared for the course team by
Tony Booth

The Open University

E242 COURSE READERS

There are two course readers associated with E242; they are:

BOOTH, T., SWANN, W., MASTERTON, M. and POTTS, P. (eds) (1992) *Learning for All 1: curricula for diversity in education*, London, Routledge (**Reader 1**).

BOOTH, T., SWANN, W., MASTERTON, M. and POTTS, P. (eds) (1992) *Learning for All 2: policies for diversity in education*, London, Routledge (**Reader 2**).

TELEVISION PROGRAMMES AND AUDIO-CASSETTES

There are eight TV programmes and three audio-cassettes associated with E242. They are closely integrated into the unit texts and there are no separate TV or cassette notes. However, further information about them may be obtained by writing to Open University Educational Enterprises Ltd, 12 Cofferidge Close, Stony Stratford, Milton Keynes MK11 1BY.

Cover illustration shows a detail of 'Midsummer Common' by Dorothy Bordass.

The Open University, Walton Hall, Milton Keynes MK7 6AA

First published 1992

Copyright © 1992 The Open University

All rights reserved. No part of this publication may be reproduced, stored in a retrieval system or transmitted, in any form or by any means, without written permission from the publisher or a licence from the Copyright Licensing Agency Limited. Details of such licences (for reprographic reproduction) may be obtained from the Copyright Licensing Agency Ltd, 90 Tottenham Court Road, London W1P 9HE.

Designed by the Graphic Design Group of The Open University

Typeset by The Open University

Printed in Scotland by Thomson Litho Ltd, East Kilbride

ISBN 0 7492 6105 6

This unit forms part of an Open University course; the complete list of units is printed at the end of this book. If you have not enrolled on the course and would like to buy this or other Open University material, please write to Open University Educational Enterprises Ltd, 12 Cofferidge Close, Stony Stratford MK11 1BY, United Kingdom. If you wish to enquire about enrolling as an Open University student, please write to the Admissions Office, The Open University, PO Box 48, Walton Hall, Milton Keynes MK7 6AB, United Kingdom.

1.1

CONTENTS

1	**Introduction**	5
	How should these units be studied?	5
2	**Starting points**	6
	An assembly	6
	Learning for all	8
	The changing contexts of education	10
	Going critical	12
	Does it matter how we talk?	13
3	**Who experiences difficulties in school?**	15
	Points of view	15
	Pupils and teachers	16
	Changing priorities	20
	Candidates for consideration?	21
	Children, young people and HIV and AIDS	21
	Children in care	25
	Devalued learners	29
	When and why is learning difficult?	32
	Defining difficulties in learning for yourself	39
	Subjects of statements	40
	Statements in practice	40
	Statements as policy	44
	A persistent culture of assessment and placement	47
	Where do they go?	49
	Assigning a category	50
	Summary	51
4	**Schools, pupils and curricula**	51
	Under the walnut tree: the Grove Primary School	53
	Curriculum and classroom support	61
	Staffing levels	63
	Policies towards children with disabilities	64
	Taking the support to pupils?	64
	Secondary transfer	66
	Impington Village College	67
	Whitmore High School	71
	A whole-school response	72

		From remedial extraction to learning support	73
		Developing mixed-ability teaching	77
	Naming the rose		80
	Summary		82
5	**Investigations**		82
		When and why is learning difficult?	83
		Care and education	83
		The story of a statement	84
		A school trip	84
		Inclusion and exclusion?	84
		How and why are students grouped?	84

Appendix 1 Who's to blame? A multi-layered epic — 84

Appendix 2 Advice on the production of statements — 95

Appendix 3 The open-air school: sunshine, rest and food — 104

Appendix 4 Bob's story — 106

References — 109

Acknowledgements — 113

1 INTRODUCTION

1.1 This unit lays the foundations for the course. It does not replace or duplicate the *Course Guide* which contains an overview of the course and how to study it. You should read that before you read this unit. Here I ask you to make connections between what you read and what you already know, and to keep in mind as you pursue the course all the interconnecting systems of education within which children and young people learn. In the next section (Section 2) I will provide some starting points for the course. Section 3 asks, 'Who experiences difficulties in school?' and examines the perspectives of teachers and pupils, the priorities we assign to the difficulties of students and the ways in which difficulties in learning can be understood. It looks at how a small percentage of pupils are officially categorized as having 'learning difficulties' through a procedure called 'statementing' in England and Wales and 'recording' in Scotland. Section 4, 'Schools, pupils and curricula', concentrates on the attempts of a primary and a secondary school to provide appropriate curricula for the diversity of their pupils within mixed groups. The unit ends with suggestions for investigations you can make into education policy and practice in your own area.

HOW SHOULD THESE UNITS BE STUDIED?

1.2 This unit represents four weeks' study time. It provides some basic information, presents a set of arguments and gives a framework within which to study chapters from the course readers and a television programme. After a short overview of the concerns of the course in the next section, there are two substantial sections (Sections 3 and 4) which will take up the bulk of your study time. I have set out below the material other than this text that will be studied in each section of the unit and where it can be found.

Section 2 Starting points

Reader 1, Chapter 32: 'Writing clearly: contributing to the ideal comprehensibility situation' by Margaret Peter.

Section 3 Who experiences difficulties in school?

Appendix 1 in this unit: 'Who's to blame? A multi-layered epic' by Dennis Mongon and Susan Hart.

Reader 1, Chapter 24: 'Affected by HIV and AIDS: cameos of children and young people' by Philippa Russell, with an introduction by Tony Booth.

Reader 1, Chapter 23: 'Adolescents, sex and injecting drug use: risks for HIV infection' by Marina Barnard and Neil McKeganey.

Reader 1, Chapter 22: 'Stressing education: children in care' by Felicity Fletcher-Campbell.

Reader 1, Chapter 11: 'In the driving seat? Supporting the education of traveller children' by Chris Mills.

Appendix 2 in this unit: 'Advice on the production of statements' by the Department of Education and Science.

Reader 2, Chapter 15: 'Ruled out or rescued? A statement for Balbinder' by Elizabeth Grugeon.

Section 4 Schools, pupils and curricula

TV1 *Under the Walnut Tree*.

Reader 2, Chapter 1: 'Under the walnut tree: the Grove Primary School' by Tony Booth.

Appendix 3 in this unit: 'The open-air school: sunshine, rest and food'.

Appendix 4 in this unit: 'Bob's story' by Dennis Mongon and Susan Hart.

Reader 1, Chapter 12: 'Chris Raine's progress: an achievement to be proud of' by Alyson Clare.

Reader 2, Chapter 2: 'A curricular response to diversity at Whitmore High School' by Christine Gilbert and Michael Hart.

Reader 1, Chapter 31: '*Le mot juste*: learning the language of equality' by Caroline Roaf.

2 STARTING POINTS

2.1 Schools contain children and young people who differ in backgrounds, attainments and interests. How should they respond to the diversity of their students?

AN ASSEMBLY

2.2 It is the start of the school day at the Grove, a primary school which you will visit again later in this unit when the pupils are a year older. A teacher has been working with her class of ten-year-olds preparing for an assembly. They have come to present an improvised morality play based on a traditional story and to read poems they have written. They start with the play.

2.3 The scene is a cottage last thing at night. A man and a woman, a couple, are arguing and it is clear that they are engaged in a familiar ritual. The front door to their house has been left open and they cannot agree whose turn it is to close it. After heated debate they agree that the first of them to speak will do it. They retire to bed.

2.4 Soon a band of thieves discovers the open door, enters the cottage and starts to remove the couple's belongings. Madeleine, one of the robbers, provides the getaway vehicle. The couple look on with open but silent mouths as chairs are piled onto Madeleine's electric wheelchair and she drives them away.

2.5 As one item after another is removed from the cottage the story begins to drag for me but the assembled pupils watch intently and laugh as the home is progressively dismantled. There is a warm and relaxed atmosphere. It's not a high pressure performance.

2.6 Finally the couple are lifted out of their bed and the burglars remove it. The husband, unable to contain himself any longer, cries out in horror, 'We've lost everything!', whereupon his wife gleefully responds, 'You spoke first, you have to close the door!' The audience claps loudly in appreciation.

2.7 Some of the pupils now read their poems. In the first batch they have punctuated alternate lines with the word 'move'. The poems are written with varying competence but the teacher encourages them equally, putting an arm round shoulders when extra support is needed to overcome first performance nerves. Gareth and Darren have written their poem together and perform it in unison:

> Move.
> I'm going to wack that ball.
> Move.
> I'm going to bowl that ball.
> Move.
> I'm going to crash that ball.
> Move.
> I'm going to hit them stumps.
> Move.
> I'm going to catch that ball.
> Move.
> Oh no you're not.
> Move.

2.8 Madeleine has produced a poem on a light-talker. She cannot talk but can communicate through her computer operated with a knee switch. A voice synthesizer presents her poem with a clipped American voice:

> Move.
> Look out I'm coming.
> Move.
> I'm coming fast.
> Move.
> I will run you over.
> Move.

2.9   Gary then steps forward beside Madeleine and rereads the poem for those who did not catch the limited amplification of the voice synthesizer. When the poems have been read and the pupils have applauded once more, the head teacher thanks the class, makes announcements and the pupils disperse for their lessons.

2.10   This glimpse of school life hints at an approach that can be taken to support the differing contributions of a class group. It is possible that my choice of a particular setting for the assembly may have made some of you feel less than at home. It was a primary example and you may have greater experience of secondary or special schools or further education, as a parent or a teacher or a student. You may be neither parent nor teacher and you may be hoping that this course doesn't get too involved in the minutiae of curricula. We will try to bear you all in mind.

2.11   Although many of you will be studying in relative isolation, I picture you as a diverse community and it is as well for you to be aware of this diversity. Besides differences of job and experience of education we recognize that you may be based anywhere in the United Kingdom. You may live in an inner city or a rural area; in Northern Ireland or Wales or Scotland or England; in Belfast, Pontypool, Dunfermline or Littleport. You may live in a house or a residential school or a prison or a barracks. We will try to turn this complexity of audience into a strength of the course, in an attempt to represent the experience of as many of you as possible. You have to be prepared to learn from experiences which are different from your own.

LEARNING FOR ALL

2.12   The course is concerned with students who experience difficulties or have disabilities in education. Some of those children and young people are seen, by themselves or others, as failing in education and some rebel noisily or silently by becoming 'disaffected' or truanting. Among those with disabilities, we include people who are deaf or have visual or physical disabilities. Like Madeleine, they may be helped by technology to gain access to a full range of subjects or they may have limited powers of communication. We are concerned with understanding and preventing difficulties in learning among school students whatever their level of attainment. Only a small proportion of such students are officially categorized as having 'learning difficulties'. We have tried to be comprehensive in our course although inevitably, in trying to cover so much ground, there are some issues which you may feel have been examined inadequately.

2.13   You will also find that at different points of the course the focus shifts. Sometimes attention is given to difficulties in learning in primary or secondary schools, at other times the main concern is with children with disabilities and their teachers and families. We will try to be clear when we are referring to a particular group of children and young people but you must watch out for switches in emphasis.

2.14   The course ranges from pre-school to further and higher education. Most of the course, however, deals with the compulsory school years. Unit 5 examines pre-school and Unit 13 is about post-16 education and training.

2.15   *Learning for All*'s focus, however, is not only, or even primarily, on the difficulties or disabilities experienced by children and young people. It is equally concerned with ways schools and curricula contribute to the creation, resolution and prevention of these difficulties. We are also interested in exploring the extent to which an attempt to make schools responsive to the difficulties in learning or disabilities of some of their students can help to make them fit places for the diversity of all their students. The course's title is a challenge to all of us to link the reduction of difficulties in learning with the development of an education system that is responsive to all learners irrespective of their gender, skin colour, background, level of attainment, abilities or disabilities. An attempt to define the practices in such a responsive system is contained in a series of books which were put together for Part B of the Advanced Diploma in Special Needs in Education: *Preventing Difficulties in Learning* (Booth, Potts and Swann, 1987), *Producing and Reducing Disaffection* (Booth and Coulby, 1987), and *Including Pupils with Disabilities* (Booth and Swann, 1987).

2.16   We recognize that we emphasize some approaches to teaching the diversity of students more than others but we are aware of the variety of responses that are made in schools and colleges. You can think of these as falling within two opposing bands. There are those who start by accepting the heterogeneous nature of learning groups and look for teaching methods, curricula, and ways of organizing resources to support and increase this diversity. Alternatively there are those who start with the assumption that learning takes place best in groups of 'similar' learners and look for ways of selecting and matching students, methods, curricula and schools.

2.17   Arguments between the proponents of these approaches have been a constant feature of education. Three related principles inform such disputes. A *comprehensive principle* is concerned with the education of pupils of diverse backgrounds and attainments together in primary and secondary schools. An *integration principle* is concerned with increasing the participation of children and young people who experience difficulties in learning or have disabilities within the mainstream of education. A *principle of equality of value* is concerned with the reduction of discrimination against children and young people in education on the basis of their background, gender, skin colour, attainments or disability. The first two of these have obvious counter principles, of *selection* and *segregation*. I would argue that selection and segregation are bound up with the ascription of differences in value to students on the basis of their background, attainment and disability. You will have ample opportunity to examine and contest this assertion.

2.18 The discussion of principles is a feature of the course since it is hard to see how intelligent decisions can be made about education if we are unaware of good reasons for them. However, the course also attempts to present you with the range of existing practices. In discussing what *should* go on in education, it is essential to have a clear idea what actually does go on as well as an understanding of why things are as they are.

THE CHANGING CONTEXTS OF EDUCATION

2.19 If the difficulties that arise in the education system are to be understood, we need to recognize the nature of that system and the sources of power within it. The system is always changing, sometimes more rapidly than at other times. You will have an opportunity to consider the changing interrelationships between central and local government, school governors, teachers and headteachers, the unions and voluntary organizations, state and private education, parents and students. Units 14 and 15 attempt that job.

2.20 In my view the largest changes to the system since I started work in education have occurred with the creation of large and remote local education authorities (LEAs) following the reorganization of local government in 1974, brought in by the 1972 Local Government Act, and then the curtailment of LEA powers with the introduction of the National Curriculum, local management of schools (LMS), and the pressures for schools to opt out of local government control brought in by the 1988 Education Reform Act. (For a fascinating account of the recent history of education see *Education and the Social Order 1940–1990* by Brian Simon, 1991.)

2.21 After the 1944 Education Act control over the curriculum in the United Kingdom was relatively loose. While there was a broad consensus about what students should learn at different stages in the system, there was variation between schools. Even so, a number of pressures kept the extent of variation in check. Most schools adopted a politically safe mix of approaches and curricula. There have been very few schools, for example, which allowed pupils to gain democratic experience in making decisions about aspects of school life, including their own curricula, for themselves. But the major constraining feature has been the examination system at 16+ and the selection procedures operating thereafter. The education system in schools might have been pictured as a funnel, broad at the point of entry, but narrowing as the point of exit approaches.

2.22 The 1988 Education Act has attempted to change the shape of the system in schools from a funnel to a cylinder. All students in state schools follow the same broad curriculum from five to sixteen for the great majority of the school week. It consists of three core subjects – English, maths and science – and seven foundation subjects – history, geography, technology, music, art, physical education, a modern language at all secondary schools and Welsh in addition for those in Wales. All schools must also provide religious education. You might well ask that if eleven subjects (three core, seven foundation and religious education) are to be universal, why not give them one label instead of three.

2.23   While I was writing this in 1991, the Department of Education and Science (DES) provided considerable detail on the way the subjects were to be divided up into attainment targets and the programmes of study that would enable attainment targets to be achieved. Schooling was divided up into four 'key stages', corresponding to ages 5–7, 7–11, 11–14, and 14–16. At the end of each stage pupils were to be assessed on ten levels for each attainment target and the results made available to parents and published to permit league tables of school achievements to be compiled.

2.24   When the Act was written, it was envisaged that there would be a number of pupils who would be exempted from all or part of the National Curriculum, either through the official 'statementing' procedures for identifying and making educational provision for 'children with learning difficulties' (see the next section) or at the request of the headteachers to the governors of a school. Subsequently, when the National Curriculum Council produced its advice on 'children with special needs', they advised against exemptions and argued that 'all pupils share the right to a broad and balanced curriculum, including the National Curriculum' (National Curriculum Council, 1989, p. 1). They pointed the way for statements to define how pupils might be given access to a broad and balanced curriculum, though as yet few of those preparing statements see their role in this light.

2.25   It remains to be seen how much of the original prescription in the 1988 Act will remain. Already, in 1991, there were moves away from complex and detailed testing of the National Curriculum attainment targets in primary schools because of the time this involves. A change of political party in government would also affect the force of the Act. The Labour Party claims that they would make curricula for subjects outside the core advisory and would stop schools opting out of local authority control. There is also the small matter of the GCSE exams. At some point soon the National Curriculum will turn sixteen, eyes blazing, fur bristling and teeth bared. Will the GCSE shuffle quietly away?

2.26   I find it useful to keep in mind the interview Margaret Thatcher gave to *The Sunday Telegraph* in March 1990, before the 'very British coup' which ousted her from power. She was seen by many to be the power behind the Education Reform Bill which preceded the Act. This was modestly titled 'The Great Education Reform Bill' and became known as GERBIL. At the time HERBILL seemed a more accurate reflection of its lineage. It is interesting therefore that the National Curriculum and testing arrangements developed in ways that were far removed from her conceptions. Will it eventually conform more closely to her view?

What the Prime Minister said

The core curriculum, so far as we have got the English one out, the mathematics and the science – now that originally was what I meant by a core curriculum.

Everyone simply *must* be trained in mathematics up to a certain standard. You must be trained in language and I would say some literature up to a certain standard, you really must. It is your own tongue.

It is not enough to be able to speak it: you must know some of the literature. And you simply must have the basic structure of science. And you must not be allowed to give them up before you are sixteen.

If you build these subjects in, they can be retrieved at any time.

Now that is to me the core curriculum. And it is so important that you simply must be tested on it. People have said to me: 'Is seven not too young to test a child?' I have said: 'Look, if a child is not reading by the time that child is seven, you have got to know, the teachers have got to know.' Quite a number of very bright children are slow at reading. But you cannot let it go longer than seven.

Going on to the other things in the curriculum, when we first started on this, I do not think I ever thought they would do the syllabus in such detail as they are doing now. Because I believe there are thousands of teachers who are teaching extremely well. And I always felt that when we had done the core curriculum, the core syllabus, there must always be scope for each teacher to use her own methods, her own experience, the things which she has learned and he or she really knows how to teach.

So I did not really feel that the core curriculum or any subject should take up all the time devoted to that subject, because otherwise you are going to lose the enthusiasm and the devotion and all of the extras that a really good teacher can give out of her own experience.

(Margaret Thatcher in an interview with *The Sunday Telegraph* reprinted in *The Times Educational Supplement*, 20 April 1990)

GOING CRITICAL

2.27 In reading the course texts, watching the television programmes and listening to the audio-cassettes you may hear a number of strong voices. However, we do not want you to treat any of them as above suspicion. We hope you will examine carefully and criticize all aspects of the course as well as questioning your own ideas and the practices in education that you encounter. We hope that by the end of the course you will have become adept at teasing out and examining the hidden assumptions and in detecting and analysing contradictions in what is said and written about education.

2.28 At the start of this section I outlined the approach of the course to difficulties in learning. I suggested that the course writers see the resolution of difficulties in learning as part of the task of creating an education system that is responsive to all learners. Is this a realistic aim? What are the limits of this approach? Are the interests of different groups of learners opposed, such that the reduction of difficulties for some involves the redirection of resources from others? If so, what principles should determine the way teaching and material resources are distributed within the systems of education? The course's title does not have a question mark. It is up to you to put one there and after any other assertion in the course.

2.29 One of my intentions in telling the story of an assembly at the start of this section was to open a dialogue with you about the way all pupils might feel equally valued as members of a school community. Is it realistic to expect people to value equally the achievements of a student who gains three grade As at A-level and the halting communication of an eighteen-year-old categorized as having severe learning difficulties? Does an attempt to make all pupils feel valued involve the curbing of excellence?

2.30 There are a number of barriers to understanding and evaluating what is going on in education and special education. We are all held back by our own limitations, by our previous convictions, by our comfort with unexamined ways of thinking that support our own needs and fantasies and our place within our culture and society. There are many reasons why challenging received wisdom may seem against our own interests. One of the students on the forerunner to this course concluded after her examination of professional power relationships that she had 'blown her chances of promotion for ever'.

Does it matter how we talk?

2.31 One of the most fascinating conceits and deceits of power is the way some people come to believe that the acquisition of power in itself confers them with knowledge and sense. In fact the reverse process may occur. If you can win an argument by virtue of your position then you may be less scrupulous about the nature of the arguments you deploy.

2.32 One of the ways people avoid holding up their ideas to scrutiny is by adopting a private or professional language which is only meant to be understood by the initiated. Jargon and acronyms are rife in education. The National Curriculum has given rise to a new crop, ironically at the same time as loud rhetoric about giving 'outsiders', particularly parents, more power in governing bodies and through choice in the 'market place'. Do most parents understand SATs, profile components and attainment targets?

2.33 Since the mid-1960s it has become increasingly common to refer to some children who experience difficulties in learning or have disabilities as having *special needs* (Webb, 1967) or *special educational needs* (DES, 1978). Many people working within education with children who experience difficulties in learning or have disabilities, think of themselves as 'special needs teachers', and you may be among them. In the next section I will explore such category systems. Does the labelling of special needs teachers and pupils help or hinder all teachers in sharing responsibility for reducing difficulties in learning? It is not easy to change the way we use language, though it is more possible to change our own than other people's. But we do find that we need a term that describes the loose amalgam of systems and concerns which comprise the subject matter of this course. Sometimes I and other course authors talk of 'special education' to indicate our focus on difficulties in learning and children with disabilities. This can have an unfortunate connotation, leading some people to think that we are concerned with special *school* education, whereas our interest is in the inclusive mainstream.

Activity 1   Gobbledegook or talking turkey?

In Reader 1, Chapter 32, Margaret Peter, editor of the *British Journal of Special Education*, has written about some of the unnecessary jargon she has encountered in surveying writing about education. Some of you may have tried to plough through impenetrable prose in an article in an educational journal, wondering why your capacity for understanding has suddenly become so deficient. Margaret Peter suggests that the fault is unlikely to be yours. As you read the chapter, consider whether your activities involve using language which excludes others from understanding them. Make a note of any parts of the chapter where you are expected to understand what is being said without sufficient information.

2.34   I feel that the message of this brief chapter is clear without further explanation from me. You may already find yourself enmeshed by the jargon of your workplace as part of a 'quality control service', for example, the new name for some LEA advisory and inspection services. You may not have the flexibility to resist jargon at work, so you can treat this course as an opportunity to escape from it – if we do our job properly.

2.35   Did you mind the echo of the beginning of *Pride and Prejudice* in the opening sentence? The return to Jane Austen with the final sentence of the chapter is neatly done but perhaps you find that literary allusions can be another way of excluding people. But it would be a pity to take this too far. We choose words in writing for a whole variety of conscious and unconscious reasons. They can fit their purpose well *and* have a more idiosyncratic derivation. The subtitle I added to the chapter you have just read, besides being an attempt to underline, in ironical fashion, the chapter's point, is also a reference to the work of Jurgen Habermas, about whom I know very little except for his suggestion that communication between people is most successful when it takes place in what he calls the 'ideal speech situation' where speakers have equal power. He is also renowned for the density of his prose. It is also a passing acknowledgement to a friend, Heather Wood, who died while she was researching the applicability of the ideas of Habermas to special education. She felt that behind the complexities of expression were gems, not of ignorance, but brilliance. Now you know. But rest assured, such reflections will be limited hereafter.

3 WHO EXPERIENCES DIFFICULTIES IN SCHOOL?

3.1 In this section I will consider the nature of the difficulties experienced by children and young people in school. I will look at the point of view from which difficulties are defined and how the priority we give to the various difficulties faced by pupils changes with their incidence or our view of their incidence, our knowledge and awareness of particular problems and our image of our roles as educators or carers.

3.2 I will then take a particular look at the problems faced by three overlapping groups of children and young people. I will discuss how young people are affected by HIV and AIDS. I will examine some of the concerns of children and young people in care. I will ask whether some groups are discriminated against or devalued within education and whether such experiences contribute to other educational difficulties. I will use as an illustrative example the experience of one teacher working with traveller children.

3.3 I will then move on to ask more specific questions about the nature of difficulties in learning. I will examine official definitions of learning difficulties and special needs, point out the difficulties with these definitions and encourage you to define difficulties in learning for yourself.

3.4 I will end the section by describing the formal assessment procedures known as 'statementing' in England and Wales and 'recording' in Scotland and ask how the procedures work in practice and the part they can play as instruments of policy.

POINTS OF VIEW

3.5 That people survey education from different perspectives which form a barrier to understanding between them is one of the major themes of this course. They may tend to share a perspective because they do a particular job or occupy a particular position in the structure of education or in the structure of society. Yet within any particular category, such as teachers or pupils or parents, there will be an array of differing views.

Pupils and teachers

3.6 If you asked pupils and teachers to identify the sources of their major difficulties in school you would get different sets of answers. You might get some surprises too. When asked to identify the major difficulty at their school, one group of teachers immediately referred to the school caretaker's policy of controlling access to the toilets and toilet paper. At another school a major dispute centred around the contents of a break-time snack. Bananas were banned from the classroom and the parents of a boy whose favourite food was bananas withdrew him from the school rather than submit to the rule of the carrot and apple (*Cambridge Evening News*, 17 September 1990).

3.7 You might find that pupils frequently identify the difficulties they have with other pupils and that teachers have considerable problems with other teachers. Bullying might be uppermost in the minds of many pupils and this is a subject that has been receiving increased attention in the United Kingdom following the very high importance it has been given in some other countries (Roland and Munthe, 1989; Lane and Tattum, 1988). We are devoting a section of Unit 11/12 to the issue as well as Television Programme 5, *Danger, Children at Play*. No forms of bullying are pleasant but sexual and racial harassment and violence represent particularly insidious forms (see Jones, 1985; Herbert, 1989; Troyna, 1990; Commission for Racial Equality, 1988). Not all bullying is between pupils. Pupils can bully teachers, teachers can bully pupils and each other. Reprinted below is one teacher's experience of being mercilessly bullied by the headteacher of her school:

Beaten by a head

I KNEW I was a good teacher and I always got on well with my pupils. There were never any discipline problems and I was proud of the fact that I didn't have to refer to the head all the time.

Then one morning, three months after a new head arrived, he walked into my class and demanded to know why I wasn't dictating notes. In front of everyone he said my teaching method was ridiculous.

The next day, when I caught him listening outside the door, he marched in and complained that I'd parked my car in the wrong slot, that I seemed to be incapable of doing anything right.

I remember the anger rising in my chest and colour flooding into my face, but I didn't want to have a shouting match in front of the whole class, so I just kept quiet.

One Monday morning he told me that he no longer had a class for me. Instead, I had to teach different groups, which meant there wasn't the same opportunity to build up a relationship with the pupils. It then became more difficult to keep control because I was always moving about.

Because I felt stateless not having a proper base, a male colleague offered me a working space in his classroom. The head went out of his way to get me removed and he kept calling my colleague into his office to convince himself that we were having an affair.

By that time the atmosphere in the staffroom was appalling. He would always have his knife into one person at a time, apart from those who sided with him to stay out of trouble.

It eventually reached the point where people didn't talk to the person whose turn it was to be bullied, in case they were seen by the head and became the target for further recriminations.

He went on endlessly putting people down and bombarding them with insults, screaming at staff during slanging matches in the corridors. What had once been a school with a lovely atmosphere deteriorated to the extent that the pupils were getting upset and parents weren't wanting to send their children there any more. The union advised us to unite and stand up against him together, but we were so divided by this time and so governed by fear it was unthinkable.

(*Guardian*, 19 June 1990, p. 25)

3.8 But teachers do have particular preoccupations of their own. They are paid to teach and to teach successfully they have to create order. Some see this order as coming from a planned and interesting curriculum while others view the maintenance of order as a separate skill of classroom management passed on from experienced staff to new recruits in tricks of the trade. A while ago I gathered a group of teachers together to discuss their views about control. They included both special school and mainstream teachers and they compared the expectations of them in their different settings. The discussion ended with the following exchange:

> MARY: We have reached the point in our school where we can admit to another member of staff including classroom assistants when we need a break from a particular pupil. You need to be able to say you have had enough just to diffuse the situation. Some days you're simply on a shorter fuse than others.
>
> MARGARET: But it can be so threatening. Of all the things people look at to see whether you're a good teacher or not, the first is always: can you keep control?
>
> CLAIRE: Teachers discuss kids in the staffroom but they also talk about each other: 'Oh she's bloody awful she shouldn't be in teaching.' You hear it being said all the time. You think to yourself I hope they never say that about me. I hope I'm not discussed when I walk out of the door. People are constantly aware of having to be seen to be the all-powerful being when they are in the classroom.
>
> Most secondary schools you are left struggling away on your own. You can send them to the head but it doesn't usually do you much good. The kids just see you as an idiot: 'Oh she's sent him to Mr so-and-so ... ' In the school for children with severe learning difficulties there simply wasn't that pressure – there were behavioural problems but no problem of en-masse control like you get in secondary schools or primary schools or the school I'm in now. There was a different attitude towards adults from the kind of pupil we had. Their difficult behaviour was something you understood. You didn't get uptight about it.
>
> MARY: And with a better teacher–pupil ratio you wouldn't be afraid all the time that one pupil would spark off another.
>
> CLAIRE: That's right, we did have seven kids with three staff. So if a kid decided to throw a wobbly or smear the walls he or she was quietly removed and calmed down and coped with. You can't do that with a class of thirty kids in a secondary school.
>
> MARGARET: And also it wasn't seen as a reflection of you.

(Booth and Hesketh, 1987, p. 6)

Activity 2   Perspectives on trouble

'Who's to blame? A multi-layered epic' by Susan Hart and Dennis Mongon is Appendix 1 in this unit. It is adapted from Chapter 2 of *Improving Classroom Behaviour: new directions for teachers and pupils* (Mongon et al., 1989). In it the authors draw on their experience of secondary teaching to attempt to describe an incident of school life from a variety of points of view of teachers and students. It is a fictionalized account but the competing and clashing views of education which it contains are intended to be authentic.

If you are not a secondary-school teacher, you may find that there are references in this appendix to a world with which you have little acquaintance. As you read it, consider the assumptions that are made about our knowledge of this world. I suggest that you also bear in mind the following questions:

- Is it desirable and/or possible for teachers in a school to have an agreed approach towards the difficulties encountered by pupils?

- What power should a specialist teacher in Mary's position have to decide how pupils like Jack and Fred are returned to mainstream lessons?

- Do some pupils become identified as troublemakers and does this increase the likelihood of their being injured innocents?

- How can the gender of pupils and teachers affect issues of discipline in a school?

3.9   In secondary schools there may be 'heads of year', 'tutors' and 'tutor groups' who are expected to keep 'journals' up-to-date. There is an emphasis on registers. There may be an 'on-site disruptive unit' in which some staff work for part of their time. Although the unit is on-site, getting to it may involve crossing a muddy field.

3.10   We are also expected to understand something about the practice of suspension or exclusion. Among other issues, the 1986 Education Act dealt with changes in the procedures for exclusion from schools. It also ended corporal punishment in state, but not private, schools in England and Wales. The word 'suspension' does not figure as a legal term. The head has the right to exclude a pupil for a fixed or indefinite time or to recommend permanent exclusion but must inform parents immediately and tell them of their right of appeal to the governing body and the LEA who both have powers to reinstate a pupil. Governors have a right to appeal against the decision of a local authority who reinstates a pupil against their wishes.

3.11   In Pilgrim Way there are clear conflicts over the way teachers should respond to pupils like Fred. Teachers can feel that a huge amount of work with a pupil can be undermined as soon as this pupil touches another point in the system. One solution to such conflicts is for a school to attempt to reach an explicit agreement between all staff, as in Whitmore High School described in the following section of this unit. Alternatively a teacher in Mary's position could be given formal responsibility for formulating the approach to be taken. In either case, the agreements can only work with the active co-operation of all the teachers concerned.

3.12   The teachers in the story differ in how they attribute responsibility for producing disruption among the actions of pupils, the behaviour of teachers and the nature of the curriculum. The appendix's authors argue that difficulties can be reduced effectively only through an examination of the way the school is organized, the nature of the curriculum and the manner of its presentation:

> As far as Fred's own 'story' is concerned, Sheila is merely acting out a symbolic role which could potentially have been filled by any representative of the school's authority. Had she acted differently, the incident might have been prevented on this occasion. But it has to be recognized that the likelihood of a confrontation that would provoke Fred's suspension occurring on another occasion would be an ever-present possibility as long as the vicious circle continued to operate, through which Fred, in turn, rejected and was rejected by his school. Our experience suggests that the crisis which occurred on Fred's return to class after a 'successful' period in the unit is typical of what so often happens. A colleague formerly working in an on-site unit for 'disruptive' pupils describes the problem as follows:
>
>> It was as though the pupil would come to us for a boost of confidence. We would spend six weeks or so healing the wounds of shattered confidence only to return the pupil to circumstances in which we could predict the scab would be picked and festered in very little time.
>>
>> Why would pupils who could work hard, behave sensitively and appear to enjoy coming to school when in the unit, behave so differently in the atmosphere of the main school? At least one pupil a year would end up expelled for their behaviour on the main site, despite the work they had put in with the unit. We were failing to prepare them for the 'real world' of school and, in retrospect, too much of our time was spent trying to teach the students strategies which might enable them to foresee or circumvent potentially difficult situations without bringing teaching staff or the pupils' peers into the process. Consequently, the emphasis for blame and remediation lay squarely on the shoulders of the referred pupil who ended up doing an awful lot of the work in isolation and out of the context of where the problems appeared to manifest themselves.
>>
>> (Tim Joyce)

Our experience of working with the many 'Freds' with whom we have come into contact over the years, suggests that as long as so much of the onus is on a pupil to adjust his or her behaviour to fit in with the school's scheme of things, the chances of successful long-term assimilation are small. If there is to be any hope of interrupting the self-reproducing process of rejection and response or preventing it from getting underway in the first place, then schools, as well as pupils, must be prepared to adapt and change. Schools must accept their own responsibility for examining *how* the dynamics of schooling may be contributing to 'problem behaviour', and *what* might be done both to ease the problems pupils are currently experiencing and, where possible, to prevent the same problems arising with the next generation of pupils.

Identifying features of schools' organisation and curricula, which might be adapted or improved to promote more constructive patterns of behaviour, is undoubtedly that much easier at one or more removes from the sometimes threatening immediacy of the classroom. Teachers like ourselves, who have chosen to work with 'problem' pupils, find that we are uniquely placed to look back in at the curriculum *from their point of view.*

(Mongon *et al.*, 1989, pp. 34–6)

3.13 Some classroom teachers would argue that as soon as the pressures of classroom teaching are relinquished it becomes impossible to understand education from *their* point of view.

Changing priorities

3.14 The attention given to the difficulties faced by pupils changes over time – both in degree and in form. On-site and off-site disruptive units as a solution to difficulties with behaviour in school grew dramatically in number in the 1970s and 1980s. We can think of two competing views of difficulties in behaviour: that they are best tackled by correcting or changing pupils or alternatively by correcting and changing teachers, schools and curricula. The rise in disruptive units is one indication that during the 1970s and 1980s the first of these views had become dominant.

3.15 Sometimes, problems which have been given relatively little consideration become a focus of concern for some teachers because of the level of media attention they receive. In the late 1980s and early 1990s a number of cases of child sexual abuse achieved notoriety in the press in Cleveland, Rochdale, Nottingham, Kent and elsewhere. Mica Nava has written an account of the media attention given to the Cleveland child sexual abuse cases which I found helpful in thinking out my own reactions (Nava, 1988; see also Doyle, 1989, and Maher, 1987). Whatever the merits of particular allegations, there is no escaping the fact that child sexual abuse is uncomfortably widespread. However, the separation of child abuse into cases of sexual and non-sexual abuse may deflect attention from the far greater number of children who suffer from the latter.

3.16 The patterns of disease and disability have clearly changed over the years. Until the 1950s, polio was a large contributor to the number of pupils with physical disabilities in the UK. Children with spina bifida entered schools in increasing numbers in the 1960s. At the end of the 1950s they represented 5 per cent of the population of schools for children with physical disabilities in London but in the 1960s 'it was not unusual ... to find that up to three-quarters of children' in such schools had spina bifida (Tew, 1987, p. 95). The change had been brought about in the main by the invention of the Spitz-Holter valve in 1958 which meant that the hydrocephalus associated with the condition could be treated and this encouraged surgeons to close the spinal lesions of children and allow them to survive.

3.17 According to Tew (1987), since the early 1970s three factors have contributed to the considerable fall in numbers of children with spina bifida in schools. There seems to have been a small drop in the prevalence of spina bifida, but more significantly, the use of amniocentesis has allowed for detection in the womb and many parents have decided to terminate the pregnancy. Finally, those doctors who were unhappy with the prospects for children with spina bifida who had received surgery won the argument for selective treatment. Since the early 1970s many children born with spinal lesions have been allowed to die, though survival rates vary depending on the precise medical policies of a particular area.

CANDIDATES FOR CONSIDERATION?

3.18 The priority we give to a particular difficulty has implications for how people concerned with the education of vulnerable pupils allocate their time and for the way resources are distributed to reduce the difficulties of students. In this sub-section I will look at three groups among the many who compete for our attention.

Children, young people and HIV and AIDS

3.19 You may find it strange that I have included material on HIV and AIDS in a course on educational difficulties. Yet children who are HIV positive are progressing through the education system and some will develop AIDS during the course of their education. Some of those who develop AIDS will die during their school days. Already children who are HIV positive have been the victims of prejudice in schools in the United Kingdom, though no-one has gone to the lengths of a judge in Florida who ordered that a six-year-old child should be kept within a glass bubble within the classroom (*The Independent*, 11 August 1988).

3.20 It is difficult to predict the priority that we will need to give in education to children and young people affected by HIV and AIDS in the United Kingdom, but we know that the epidemic is progressing rapidly in some areas within the adult population: 'In Inner London the rates of seropositivity [the presence in the blood of HIV antibodies] among sexually active women are doubling every twelve months; if this rate of increase continues the figures will soon approach those of New York and other United States cities' (*The Lancet*, 1991, p. 1572).

3.21 AIDS is already the leading cause of death among women aged 25 to 40 in New York (Chin, 1990). Government statisticians at the Department of Health are guarded about the trends for children. Nevertheless, apart from those children and young people who are HIV positive themselves, many more live with the stress of having a parent or other relative who has HIV infection or AIDS. There were 345 children aged fourteen or under in the United Kingdom who were known to have been infected with HIV-1 virus up to the end of April 1991. Of these 33 had died.

Activity 3   Affected by HIV and AIDS

Now read Chapter 24 in Reader 1, 'Affected by HIV and AIDS: cameos of children and young people' by Philippa Russell. As you read the chapter consider the impact that HIV and AIDS is likely to have on the support that children may need in school. The situation will change with the life of this course. Your knowledge of up-to-date statistics and educational practices may enable you to use the reading to reflect on the changes that have occurred.

3.22 The incidence of HIV and AIDS in some parts of the world, particularly sub-Saharan Africa, will stretch and swamp adult and child welfare services in the coming years. Since I wrote the introduction to the chapter, more information has become available about the transmission of HIV and the progression from HIV to AIDS that will affect predictions about children with HIV and AIDS in school in the United Kingdom. There is unlikely to be much increase in numbers affected by contaminated blood as blood products are now treated effectively in the UK. The transmission rate between mothers and their newborn babies is being revised downwards. According to the European Collaborative Study, only 13 per cent of babies born to mothers who are HIV positive remain HIV positive themselves. All of these babies are born with antibodies to HIV in their blood but most are not infected with the virus (European Collaborative Study, 1991). The authors of this report remain undecided about whether transmission of the virus takes place within the uterus or at delivery. A number of studies agree that in the developed world the progression from HIV to AIDS takes place in approximately 50 per cent of people within ten years, though there is variation with age (Lee, 1990). Older people tend to progress from HIV to AIDS more rapidly. Babies may progress very rapidly indeed. 30 per cent of those babies who are infected with the virus develop AIDS within the first six months of life (European Collaborative Study, 1991). There is increasing evidence that zidovudine (AZT) and other drugs, particularly in combination, retard the onset of AIDS and this has implications for testing policies and speed of intervention particularly with babies. Only one-fifth of the number of mothers discovered to be HIV positive in a London study by testing for antibodies in their newborn babies were known to be HIV positive before testing. Questions can be raised about the ethics of such anonymous testing which did not permit particular individuals to be identified, informed and offered treatment (Ades *et al.*, 1991).

Growing up gay

3.23 Young people growing up gay may feel particular pressures since in the United Kingdom and other developed nations the initial spread of HIV infection was largely in gay men and this added to prejudice about gay people. Their position within education was made more difficult by Section 28 of the Local Government Act 1988 which was inspired by fears within government that attempts within some local authorities to counter discrimination against gays and lesbians were undermining family life. Section 28 states:

> A local authority shall not:
>
> (a) intentionally promote homosexuality or publish material with the intention of promoting homosexuality;
>
> (b) promote the teaching in any maintained school of the acceptability of homosexuality as a pretended family relationship.

3.24 While the notion of 'a pretended family relationship' has never been defined, the clause has been taken by some people to imply that teachers should not attempt to counter discrimination against gay and lesbian people by arguing that homosexuality is part of the normal range of human sexual expression. Rogers (1989) has argued that the law does not imply this. It applies to local authorities, not teachers, and school policies on sex education are the responsibility of governing bodies rather than LEAs. Rogers argues that if teachers follow the guidance of school governors rather than acting under pressure from their LEA, it is 'highly unlikely' that they could be disciplined for teaching that homosexual relationships could be part of the variety of family life. He draws attention to the advisory force of Department of Education and Science Circular, November 1989, which argues that: 'There is no place in any school in any circumstances for teaching which advocates homosexual behaviour, which presents it as the "norm", or which encourages homosexual experimentation by pupils'. However, Rogers argues that presenting something as the 'norm' is not the same as treating it as 'normal':

> Tutors should not be discouraged from discussing homosexuality generally, as one of a range of lifestyles, nor specifically in relation to HIV and AIDS … Tutors should not 'promote' homosexuality. But

no tutor would encourage pupils to be homosexual or to 'experiment' with homosexuality – or any other sexual practice. Discussing or explaining a practice or form of behaviour is neither promoting nor advocating it.

(Rogers, 1989, p. 38)

HIV and drug use

3.25 Because HIV infection can be passed on by infected blood, the sharing of needles by injecting drug users is a major way in which the infection has spread in the United Kingdom. The infection is then spread further by sexual partners of injecting drug users with HIV infection. In areas of the country where injecting drug use is high, young people who have unprotected sex are at particular risk. One of the central messages of education about HIV and AIDS is that 'there are no high-risk groups, only high-risk behaviours'. Are young people continuing to put themselves at risk?

Activity 4 Young people at risk?

Now read 'Adolescents, sex and injecting drug use: risks for HIV infection', by Marina Barnard and Neil McKeganey (Reader 1, Chapter 23). As you read the chapter consider the following general and specific issues:

(a) Are you satisfied with the methods for gaining information from the young people and that they yielded accurate information?

(b) What picture do you get of the students' world outside school? What effects might this have on the approach taken towards education by pupils and teachers?

(c) What are the risks for HIV infection of these students? Imagine two scenarios. Think of a girl or boy who starts injecting drugs by sharing a needle. Think of a girl or boy who has unprotected sex with a person with HIV. What circumstances lead to these two young people putting themselves at risk?

My responses are:

(a) The authors do not say whether parents of the young people were informed that a research project was taking place within the school. Should their consent have been sought?

(b) I find the chapter informative and clear. The area is economically poor and the pressures for drug use are high but there is a strong sense of community. It is a setting in which teachers may be tempted to have low expectations for students and where students may have a limited view of the possibilities for their future. These are issues to which I will return in Unit 11/12.

(c) Some of us may feel reluctant to consider the details of the scenarios I suggested. Embarrassment about sexual intercourse or the use of condoms is not confined to young people, nor, of course, is engaging in risky unprotected sex. To have a realistic chance of understanding and tackling these issues with young people we may have to acknowledge and confront our own feelings and behaviour.

It is easy to use language about HIV and AIDS that is inaccurate or offends or discriminates against people with HIV or AIDS. The chart in Figure 1 (overleaf) provides some guidelines on terms to use and avoid.

Children in care

3.27 In French schools, teachers pay less attention to the emotional and physical welfare of pupils than do teachers in the United Kingdom where a concern for pupils' difficulties encompasses a far wider range of issues than teaching methods and materials. The emphasis on welfare in British schools has been challenged by some who believe that there should be a strict demarcation between teaching and social work. An awareness of the social and emotional stresses on children, it is argued, can lead to insufficient emphasis on educational progress. This is precisely the point made below by Felicity Fletcher-Campbell in the case of children who are in care.

3.28 Children in care are one of the most vulnerable groups in society and education. They are a relatively small group. At 66,000, they are about half the size of the group currently in special schools. The great majority are in foster homes. Attention has been focused in the media on the remaining group in children's homes because of the high profile given to investigations of child sexual abuse and abuses of power by the 'carers' in social services departments.

Activity 5   A concern for education

While we were preparing this course we were contacted by Felicity Fletcher-Campbell of the National Foundation for Educational Research because she was concerned that we might omit a discussion of the educational vulnerability of children in care. We asked her to write a short chapter setting out her thoughts on the education of children in care which we have included as Chapter 22 in Reader 1. As you read the chapter consider a list of questions you would wish to ask to find out whether a group of six young people in a small children's home were being educated appropriately. Whom would you wish to talk to?

Terms to avoid	Why?	Use instead
• Carrying AIDS • AIDS carrier • AIDS positive	This confuses the two distinct phases of being infected with HIV and having AIDS. People 'have' AIDS, they don't 'carry' it.	*HIV antibody positive* *People with HIV*
• AIDS test	The most commonly used test detects antibodies to HIV. There cannot be a test for AIDS, as this depends on a diagnosis according to clinical symptoms.	*HIV antibody test*
• AIDS virus	Can easily cause confusion between HIV and AIDS unless used with caution.	*HIV (Human Immuno-deficiency Virus)*
• Catching AIDS	It isn't possible to catch AIDS. It is possible to catch HIV, but even this is misleading as it suggests transmission is similar to colds or flu.	*Contract HIV* *Become HIV positive*
• Full blown AIDS	When the correct distinction between HIV and AIDS is made, there is no need to use the term 'full blown AIDS'.	*AIDS*
• AIDS sufferer	Having AIDS doesn't mean being ill all the time. Someone with AIDS may continue to work and live a normal life after diagnosis. 'Sufferer' is therefore inappropriate.	*Person with AIDS*
• Plague	Plague suggests a contagious disease, which AIDS is not.	*Epidemic*
• Innocent victim	Suggests anyone else with AIDS is guilty.	
• High risk groups	It is clear that there is risk behaviour, not risk groups. Classification as a member of any particular group does not put anyone at greater risk.	

Figure 1 Talking about HIV and AIDS (ACTUP (Aids Coalition to Unleash Power), London)

3.29 I would wish to discuss the children's education with teachers, social workers and childcare workers in the children's home as well as the children themselves. The following questions are some of those to which I would hope to obtain answers:

- Who has responsibility for ensuring that the young people receive appropriate education and what steps do they take to fulfil this role?
- Is there good contact between home and school?
- Does a particular person in the children's home make time to discuss the school day, to give support and help with homework?
- Do the teachers and childcare workers respect the ordinary rights of the young people to privacy?
- What steps are taken to maximize educational continuity?
- What steps are taken to encourage the young people, their teachers and careworkers to have high expectations for educational attainment?

3.30 A list of questions such as this can make the issues seem simplistic. Like anyone else a young person in care has complex needs for emotional support and encouragement and an intelligent recognition and assessment of the best way for them to progress in education. Felicity Fletcher-Campbell argues that because young people in care have other pressing needs their education may be overlooked. However, it is clear from the testimony of young people and from reports on their care that their basic human rights may be overlooked too and that this may make it a far from simple matter to increase attention on their education.

Pinning down the problems in care

3.31 In 1979, Barbara Kahan published a book called *Growing up in Care* which was based on taped discussions between ten adults about their experiences in care between 1942 and 1969 (Kahan, 1979). The group identified the same problems in education as those identified by Felicity Fletcher-Campbell:

> They recognized very clearly that their attitude to school had been related to where they were living and whether the adults caring for them were concerned about their educational progress. Barry described how when he was in a children's home he was fifth from the bottom of the class of over forty, but when he was boarded out his class results got better each term until he was third from the top. He could not explain why this had happened except that his foster mother and an older boy in the family had both taken an interest in his progress and encouraged him in a variety of ways, some direct, others indirect.
> (Kahan, 1979, p. 150)

3.32 In 1991 Barbara Kahan was co-author of a report into childcare practices in Staffordshire (Kahan and Levy, 1991). This centred on an investigation into 'pin down', a system of control involving solitary confinement practised in four of the county's children's homes between 1983 and 1989.

> In the most extreme form of pin down, youngsters were deprived of all possessions and clothing except underwear, nightwear and dressing gowns; they were required to stay in a bedroom night and day, knocking on the door for permission to go the toilet; they were deprived of all contact with other residents, refused magazines, music, television, cigarettes or telephone calls; they were denied education and, sometimes, any reading or writing materials; and they were required to get up at 7.00 am and go to bed at 7.00 pm after a bath.
>
> At least 132 youngsters, a figure the report describes as probably conservative, were subjected to the regime. Of these, 81 were boys and 51 girls. One was kept in continuous pin down for 84 days; another was put in twelve times when aged between eleven and fourteen; two others, one boy and one girl, were put in when they were nine.
>
> (*Guardian*, 31 May 1991, p. 2)

One of the most disturbing features of the report is that the regime appeared to be widely known among staff within Staffordshire Social Services and its practices were openly logged. As one entry remarked: 'Another week of solitary confinement for X has had some rather peculiar effects. He is talking to himself a great deal and we have had tears several times during the course of the week' (*Guardian*, 31 May 1991, p. 2).

3.33 Following the report, the problems of children in care were highlighted in the media for a while. It was argued that with the increase in fostering many of the children who remained in care were those who had problems which made them difficult to look after:

> Ironically, some might say scandalously, these most 'challenging' young people are often in the care of the least experienced and most poorly-trained social workers.
>
> Because they are in a declining sector of social work, residential children's homes find it difficult to retain trained staff. As homes close, opportunities for promotion disappear and staff often leave after qualification for better prospects. Only one in five of those working in residential children's homes have a social work qualification. Their wages and conditions are significantly worse than those in field social work.
>
> (*The Times Educational Supplement*, 7 June 1991, p. 6)

These problems of staffing have been apparent for decades yet little is done to provide appropriate rewards and training for one of the most difficult and responsible jobs within social services.

3.34   Many of the children and young people in care attend boarding schools for students categorized as having emotional and behavioural difficulties, like Wilburton Manor, mentioned later in this unit and looked at in greater detail in Unit 11/12. Even these young people cannot be guaranteed respect. The head of one private boarding special school, Castle Hill in Shropshire, was jailed for twelve years for sexually abusing eight of his pupils (*The Times Educational Supplement*, 7 June 1991, p. 8).

3.35   The danger of pupils in boarding schools being subjected to sexual abuse was recognized with the setting up of a helpline for pupils at risk. The irony of such abuses is that sexual abuse by parents is a major reason for children being taken into care. This is a route to care that Felicity Fletcher-Campbell fails to mention. Yet, as the *Observer* reported,

> Nottingham Social Services Department discovered that 48 of the 380 children in its residential homes had been sexually abused.
>
> Most were in care because of sexual abuse, but they were found to be suffering further abuse from other residents. Six young people were said to have been abused for the first time by other children in the homes.
>
> (*Observer*, 2 June 1991, p. 4)

The findings in Nottingham were said by the Director of Social Services there to be symptomatic of 'a crisis in residential care … it is increasingly difficult to control the behaviour of children in care all of the time. The daily demands of working in this sector stretch even the most skilled and experienced staff' (*Observer*, 2 June 1991, p. 4). The Director of Oxfordshire Social Services, however, argued that ordinarily practice was good: 'Let me make a plea for the vast majority of homes that don't run penal regimes, don't beat children and offer lots of love and affection' (*Observer*, 2 June 1991, p. 4).

3.36   What are the problems of children in care? What is provision like in your area? Such questions could form the basis of an investigation later in the course.

Devalued learners

3.37   Discrimination against people because of their skin colour or gender or disability or attainment is rife in society and in education. If you are not aware of this, then reading may help you, but the best evidence is out there in the world that you encounter every day. For some people, reading may actually obscure their understanding. Writing in *The Times Educational Supplement*, Anthony Flew takes issue with the idea in the Commission for Racial Equality's (CRE) code of practice, that racism accounts for the over-representation of black students in school suspension figures:

> The code expresses concern 'over the number of ethnic minority pupils being suspended, particularly those of Afro-Carribean origin' and reports findings that in Birmingham 'black pupils were four times more likely to be suspended than white pupils'. But the CRE

> never as much as entertains the thought that the true explanation of this disparity may lie in actual differences – differences which are themselves no doubt culturally rather racially determined – between the behaviour of members of the racial sets thus compared.
>
> (Flew, 1990, p. 23)

The causes of a student's actions are often complex; they may be part of a 'multi-layered epic' as we saw in Fred's story. Yet it seems from this quotation that Flew 'never as much as entertains the thought that' racism may itself contribute to real differences in behaviour as well as to a bias in its interpretation and the reaction to it. The latter processes have been carefully documented in the study by Sally Tomlinson (1981). The prevalence of racism in education is described in the Swann, Eggleston and Macdonald Reports (DES, 1985a; Eggleston *et al.*, 1985; Macdonald *et al.*, 1989).

3.38 Discrimination against women has been documented in a vast literature in the last twenty years. One of the most visible manifestations of sexism in education is the over-representation of men in positions of power (De Lyon and Widdowson-Migniuolo, 1989; Acker, 1989). Others have documented the sexual harassment of girls as well as the difficulties that teachers have in paying as much attention to girls as to boys in classroom discussion (Herbert, 1989; Pye, 1990).

3.39 The use of ability to rank pupils is discussed further at the end of the next section. The devaluation of pupils relative to others creates and replenishes a pool of potential disaffection in schools. Whether or not the potential is realized may depend on a number of factors, not least on the efficiency of methods of control. I will return to these issues in Unit 11/12, *Happy Memories*. For the moment I hope I have done enough to provoke you into thinking about them.

Traveller children

3.40 Traveller children and their families have been and continue to be subjected to prejudice outside and inside schools. More than 250,000 travellers lost their lives under the Nazi occupation of Europe (Liegeois, 1987). In analysing English books for children published between 1914 and 1984, Dennis Binns suggested that there was no other group 'so constantly maligned and misrepresented' (Binns, 1984).

3.41 The term 'traveller' can encompass a whole variety of groups of people. It includes gypsies, fairground and circus people, new age travellers, in fact anyone who adopts a nomadic lifestyle or has previously adopted one. Kenrick and Bakewell (1990) identify five main culturally distinct groups of gypsies in the UK, of whom Romanies form the largest group (about 50,000 people according to Kenrick and Bakewell). Estimates of total numbers of travellers in the UK varies with the source. An upper figure of 110,000 is given in Liegeois (1987) and the lowest figure of 30,000 by HMI (DES, 1985b).

3.42 Dennis Binns has written about the history of travellers' education and has traced the competing attitudes towards them. He records the efforts to have the children of travellers removed from their families at the turn of the century: 'The ranks of the criminal classes are largely recruited from our vagrant population, and it is due to the state that steps should be taken to cut off that source of supply by removing children from a vicious environment' (Adams, 1898, quoted in Binns, 1990, p. 253).

3.43   The Children Act of 1908 gave powers of arrest to the police if there was a suspicion that a school-age child of a traveller was not attending school: 'Any constable who finds a person wandering from place to place and taking a child with him may ... apprehend him without a warrant, and may take the child to a place of safety' (Children Act 1908, clause 118). It was recognized that the need for casual farm labour in the summer months might involve people in travelling, but to be exempt from prosecution from April to September a traveller had to have 'obtained a certificate of having made not less than 200 attendances at a public elementary school during the months of October to March immediately preceding' (Children Act 1908, clause 118). Binns quotes an anonymous article which argued against the punitive sentiments in the Children Act 1908 and offered a basis for the education of traveller children: 'Reformers must seek, not to adapt the Gypsies to an imperfect educational system which happens to exist, but to remould that system to fit the manner of the life of the Gypsies.' (Binns, 1990, p. 254.)

3.44   However, seventy years on, in a study of a secondary school intriguingly entitled *Catch 22 Gypsies* (Ivatts, 1975), the presence of traveller children was seen by many staff as a disruption to school routine: 'Many senior members of staff are of the opinion that the school cannot offer them anything in the present situation. The children "beat the system every time" and "if you give them an inch they take a yard" and in most ways are "out of tone with the school" (Ivatts, 1975, p. 14). The school was particularly concerned about uniform and teachers appeared affronted that the traveller pupils might not assign it the same value as themselves: 'Another facet of behaviour which identifies the Gypsies as a disruptive and uncooperative group is the persistent failure to wear school uniform ... the wearing of jewellery is also against school rules and periodic purges usually hit the Gypsies hard with their liking for precious metal, rings and earrings' (Ivatts, 1975, p. 13).

Activity 6   In the driving seat

Now read 'In the driving seat? Supporting the education of traveller children' by Chris Mills (Reader 1, Chapter 11). In it, Chris Mills describes her work as a support teacher, attempting to make schools more responsive to the needs of traveller children and to counteract prejudice towards them. As you read it try to examine your own feelings towards traveller children and their families. Make a list of the efforts a school community might make to attract the traveller children in its area into school. How would you start?

3.45 You may have a number of imaginative ideas about how to make welcome within a school a group of visitors to an area or longer-term traveller residents of a designated site. Should teachers and students visit travellers in their homes? Most of my suggestions fall within the heading of staff attitudes, student attitudes and curriculum resources.

3.46 The traveller lifestyle should be visible within the books and curriculum materials of the school. There are pressures in the 1980 and 1988 Education Acts for schools to move away from the idea that they serve a particular catchment area. Within these Acts, the ideas of parental choice and open enrolment are an encouragement to schools to seek to attract parents from beyond their immediate areas. However, in many schools teachers continue to see themselves as having responsibility for education in a particular community. They would have to see themselves in this way if they were to be motivated to attract the traveller children in their community. The staff would need to agree that traveller children were to be actively encouraged to attend the school and prejudices of staff would need to be aired and overcome. The multicultural adviser or advisory teacher of staff in another school with successful experience of working with traveller children might be recruited to help at this stage. The pupils too would need to be encouraged to be welcoming to visitors to the school who might stay for varying periods of time.

Activity 7 What do you see?

Figure 2 is taken from a book called *Darwin for Beginners* (Miller and van Loon, 1982). It was used to help to explain why people fail to see facts that are staring them in the face. Jonathan Miller's argument was that the facts to support a theory of evolution were there to be recognized and interpreted by Darwin and others long before the theory of natural selection was composed. Look at the series of drawings and remarks.

Now look again at the central picture. What does this suggest about attitudes to women, old people and travellers?

What prevents us from seeing prejudice when it is staring us in the face?

WHEN AND WHY IS LEARNING DIFFICULT?

3.47 The way we approach difficulties in learning may depend on the questions we ask and the way we phrase them. The question in the heading above seems inclusive. It could be asked of any pupil in a school or anyone out of it and calls for a wide range of answers in terms of the mood and other characteristics of a learner, the nature of curricula, teaching approaches and teachers and the nature of the setting in which learning is taking place. Robert Hull sat in on a physics lesson given to

Figure 2 (Miller and van Loon, 1982, p. 8).

an O-level group. (This was before the advent of the GCSE.) The pupils clearly struggled and it is not too difficult to understand their problem:

> TEACHER: We're going to start today doing radioactivity.
>
> (This was announced amidst noise and talk.)
>
> PUPIL 1: Have you got my book, sir?
>
> PUPIL 2: What's the date?
>
> PUPIL 3: Have you got my book, sir?
>
> And there were other questions as the teacher wrote on the board: 'Introduction – radioactivity'.
>
> PUPIL 4: Is radioactivity all one word?
>
> (It was evidently to be a note-dictating session.)
>
> TEACHER: Now I'm going to start by talking a minute about the atom.
>
> PUPIL 5: Radioactivity's hyphenated.
>
> PUPIL 2: S'not!
>
> TEACHER: Now, who knows anything about the atom?
>
> PUPIL 6: Molecule.
>
> (Indistinct; the only reply.)
>
> TEACHER: Who knows anything about the structure of the atom?
>
> (No reply.)
>
> TEACHER: No? (Pause.) Well, an atom is made up of a nucleus with a positive charge, and around it it has a field of negative charge … the nucleus is very small … you could compare it with the size of a pea on the centre spot of Wembley Stadium … So an atom is mostly … ? (Pause.) What's in between?
>
> PUPIL 7: Air.
>
> TEACHER: Air is made up of atoms … What's in [indistinct]?
>
> PUPIL 5: How do you split them?
>
> TEACHER: We're interested in …
>
> PUPIL 5: How did they find out about the nucleus and [indistinct]?
>
> TEACHER: It would take too long to tell … it would take half a term in the sixth form. (Noise.) All right, then … there was this chap called Rutherford … he produced a sheet of atoms of [indistinct].
>
> PUPIL 5: How?
>
> TEACHER: … and bombarded it with particles.
>
> PUPIL 5: *Where* did he [bombard them?]
>
> TEACHER: Well, it would take a long time.
>
> ALL PUPILS: Half a term in the sixth form!
>
> (Small chorus.)

Some of what was said in this discussion was indistinct, but the dramatic shape of the passage, the urgency of the questions, and the continuous, rather grudging, redefinition of content as it reflects the teacher's priorities (in particular his need to cope), seem clear.

PUPIL 2: How did he get the atoms off it?

TEACHER: He knocked them …

PUPIL 2: (interrupting) *HOW?!!* How did he get them …

TEACHER: Well …

PUPIL 2: I want to KNOW!

(Voice rising in exasperation.)

TEACHER: Jane!

After this small explosion his exposition went on for a short while uninterrupted by questions, or anything else.

TEACHER: They thought an atom was just solid, but because … [indistinct] they found that 99 per cent went straight through, 0.9 per cent got deflected, but 0.1 per cent got bounced straight back.

PUPILS TOGETHER: Cor!

TEACHER: They couldn't explain it … they thought the only reason could be … the mass was concentrated at one particular point … if all the rest went through [indistinct] … RIGHT, so we have …

PUPIL 8: (interrupting) Is that splitting the atom?

TEACHER: No, we'll get on to that later.

The teacher then rather abruptly started his dictation of notes.

TEACHER: … small heavy particle, positively charged. It was found that if you shot particles at a nucleus, it would break up. It was found that there were two types of particles, neutrons and protons …

PUPIL 8: So the nucleus [indistinct]?

TEACHER: Well, yes, we'll see …

The note-taking was completed two minutes or so later with the words: 'surrounding this are electrons in constant motion'. Immediately, a pupil spoke:

PUPIL 9: Do they go round?

TEACHER: Yes, but it's not as simple as that, because they behave both as particles and as waves – it's a very complex part of chemistry.

ALL PUPILS: Half a term in the sixth form?

(Small chorus.)

PUPIL 5: University.

(Hull, 1985, p. 121–3)

I have been reminded of the refrain 'It would take half a term in the sixth form' every time I suggest to you that a topic will be covered in detail elsewhere in this course.

3.48 But commonly we ask questions about difficulties in learning which take us down a different path. Who has learning difficulties? The traditional way of thinking about difficulties in learning is to see them as a characteristic of particular pupils and this is encouraged by the definitions of learning difficulties and special educational needs and provision in the Education Act 1981. The rhetoric or received wisdom of special education can appear particularly authoritative because of the way it is taken up and repeated in a number of publications. Sometimes it takes its authority from a view expressed in a particular government publication, though often such sources regurgitate, in circular fashion, a prevailing view.

3.49   It has been customary to refer to the '2 per cent of pupils attending special schools' even though this over-estimates the proportion of pupils attending special schools by at least 50 per cent. People talk of the 2 per cent of pupils who are the subject of statements with no greater accuracy (see below). It has also become widely accepted that a further 18 per cent of pupils should be regarded as having 'special needs' in schools – a figure attributed to the Warnock Report, the report of the Committee of Enquiry into the Education of Handicapped Children and Young People, set up in 1973 by Margaret Thatcher (then Secretary of State for education) and chaired by Mary Warnock, which reported in 1978 (DES, 1978). Caroline Gipps, Harriet Gross and Harvey Goldstein called their book about 'children with special needs in primary schools', *Warnock's Eighteen Per Cent* (Gipps, Gross and Goldstein, 1987). Yet the number of pupils we regard as having 'learning difficulties' or 'special needs' is essentially arbitrary, depending on the nature of our definitions. The Warnock Report itself relied heavily on earlier studies of prevalence rates in which difficulties were defined in terms of a statistical difference from a mean or average. In such circumstances the number of pupils who have difficulties is a statistical invention rather than a discovery. One of the 1981 Act's definitions of learning difficulty states that children have learning difficulties if they have 'significantly greater difficulties in learning than the majority of children of [their] age'. To how many pupils might this refer? In Scotland an official report on the nature of learning difficulties in schools suggested that up to 50 per cent of pupils might have difficulties, largely because the curriculum they received was inappropriate (SED, 1978).

3.50   If placing a figure on the number of pupils who have difficulties in learning is essentially silly or arbitrary, why do people do it? I believe there are several reasonably sensible answers to this question. Discussions about educational difficulties are still dominated by a medical analogy with sick and healthy bodies which produces a view of abnormal and normal learners. It makes sense to know *how many* people are HIV-antibody positive and it will make increasing sense to know *who* is HIV-antibody positive if treatments are effective. However, I would argue that the medical analogy applied to learning which focuses our attention on the deficiencies of learners is a distraction from the task of finding appropriate curricula and teaching approaches for diverse groups.

3.51   It has also been argued that the identification of a large number of students with special needs is in the interests of those who work in the special education system and who wish to mark out a sizeable territory as their sphere of influence. Others have offered further reasons for discovering large numbers of pupils with special needs. The learning difficulties of pupils can absolve schools from the responsibility for failing to teach them. In an economy with rising unemployment it may be useful for governments to identify a large section of the population whose deficiencies are thought to make it difficult for them to cope with paid work.

Activity 8 Definitions in the Education Act 1981

Since the 1981 Act's definitions of learning difficulties and special needs are part of the legal framework of education many people feel they must think about the issues only in those terms. I will suggest that the definitions are confusing to say the least. I believe they are worth examining in some detail even if some of you find such close attention to them rather tedious. Let's start with the definition of 'special educational needs':

> A child has 'special educational needs' if he has a learning difficulty which calls for special educational provision to be made for him.
> (Education Act 1981, Section 1(1) – the definitions make no concession to non-sexist language).

Special educational needs are defined here in terms of learning difficulties and special educational provision. Although it is the first definition given in the Act, a good editor would have put it after the other two. Presumably only some of the pupils who have learning difficulties have special educational needs, otherwise why include both terms? Are the particular learning difficulties which call for (cry out for?) special educational provision characterized by their persistence and/or severity?

> A child has a learning difficulty if:
> (a) he has a significantly greater difficulty in learning that the majority of children of his age.
> (b) he has a disability which either prevents or hinders him from making use of educational facilities of a kind generally provided in schools, within the area of the local authority concerned, for children of his age.
> (Education Act 1981, Section 1(2))

Look at the first of these paragraphs. How many pupils have learning difficulties on this definition? How much greater is 'significantly greater'? Can one have a learning difficulty on some tasks and not others? It is hard to give meaning to the notion of a learning difficulty which doesn't relate to particular tasks. The notions of special educational needs and learning difficulty might have been thought to replace the past practice of determining the need for special provision in terms of general intelligence and disability. But in leaving a notion of a general learning difficulty, the term looks like a euphemism for the general incompetence thought to be measured by intelligence tests.

Now look at the second paragraph. Here we discover that some children who have disabilities have learning difficulties. These are not related to a general lack of proficiency or lack of proficiency at particular tasks but whether or not the facilities made generally available are suitable for a child in a wheelchair or who has a visual impairment or is deaf. What is the nature of a learning difficulty if a child cannot mount the stairs of a school in their wheelchair and who has it?

> 'Special educational provision' means:
>
> (a) in relation to a child that has attained the age of two years, educational provision that is additional to, or otherwise different from, the educational provision made generally for children of his age in schools maintained by the local education authority concerned.
>
> (Education Act 1981, Section 1(3))

Presumably special educational provision is to be contrasted with ordinary educational provision. If schools are staffed and resourced so that they routinely cater for the diversity of their pupils, does the notion of special educational provision disappear? Or is it limited to the atypical provision made centrally in particular mainstream or special schools?

> a child is not to be taken as having a learning difficulty solely because the language (or form of the language) in which he is ... taught is different from a language (or form of a language) which has at any time been spoken in his home.
>
> (Education Act 1981, Section 1(4))

If a learning difficulty can be attributed to an unfamiliarity with the language of instruction then a child doesn't have one, even though they would be covered by the Act's definition of learning difficulty itself. The tortuousness of this logic needs explanation. Why would we want to hold back from saying that a child whose first language is not English and who is struggling with learning has a learning difficulty? My own view on the answer to this question is that it provides a key to understanding part of what special education has been and continues to be about. Saying that a child has a learning difficulty or has special needs is not just a neutral description which helps to enable an appropriate education to be provided for them. It also confers a label which carries negative connotations of mental or physical imperfection. But if we should avoid negatively labelling pupils whose first language is not English, shouldn't we do this for all pupils?

The law tells us that a local education authority should have regard for: 'the need for ensuring that special educational provision is made for pupils who have special educational needs' (Education Act 1981, p. 2). If we substitute the Act's earlier definition of special educational needs, this statement says that *special educational provision should be made for pupils with learning difficulties which call for special educational provision to be made for them*. How are parents and practitioners meant to communicate about such ideas?

And what about the conundrum which surfaces on page 3, Section 4 of the Act, that there is a sub-group of pupils who have 'special educational needs which call for the local education authority to determine the special educational provision to be made for them'? These are the group of pupils whom it is recommended should be the subject of special multi-disciplinary assessment procedures which lead to the production of a statement of special educational needs. Try substituting the definition of special educational needs in terms of learning difficulties in the definition of this group.

We find that *statements of special educational needs are to be written for pupils who have learning difficulties which call for special educational provision to be made for them which call for the authority to determine the special provision that should be made for them!*

While this formula is plainly nonsensical it is a crucial feature of the legislation. It is the legal basis for decisions about whom should have a statement and sets the tone for relationships between local authority officers, professionals, and parents.

Defining difficulties in learning for yourself

3.52   I will have more to say about the procedures for producing statements below. But, faced with this lead from government which provides us with an absurd set of definitions, you have no choice but to construct your own view of difficulties in learning. My own way of viewing difficulties in learning is to see them as indicating a lack of match between pupils (people?) and tasks. They are not something that pupils *have* irrespective of what they are learning. They indicate a breakdown in the relationship between students and curricula. This does not mean that some people are not better at learning particular things than others, or that some people are not incompetent at many or most things. But it does direct us to find ways of providing material which is appropriate to the capacities and interests of pupils rather than towards the identification of failing pupils. This is another reason, apart from the wish to distance myself from official definitions, why I tend to write of pupils who experience difficulties in learning rather than pupils who *have* learning difficulties, even if this does seem pedantic.

3.53   My response to the notion of 'special educational needs' is to avoid its use because of the confusions that surround it. However, others, outside my immediate colleagues, categorize me as working on 'special needs' and I do not spend countless conversations trying to argue that they should use different language. Although I believe that the idea of the 'special needs child' discriminates negatively against a large group of children, there seems little immediate possibility of countering the prevailing view or ideology that it discriminates positively.

3.54   One way to exhibit the relationship between difficulties and curricula is to regard 'special needs' as 'unmet needs'. However, while this may clarify the term 'special', it does not avoid the problems with the word 'need'. I need food but I may also be said to need 'taking down a peg or two' or a child may be said to need 'a good hiding', an assertion that says more about the wishes and satisfactions of its producer than its beneficiary. The 'needs' in 'special needs' are not biological like hunger nor uncontentiously satisfied as by providing food. When professionals talk of the discovery of special needs, they mislead us from seeing their part in defining what is in a child's best interests.

SUBJECTS OF STATEMENTS

3.55 A statement of special educational needs may be produced, then, as a result of the assessment process set out in Section 5 of the Education Act 1981. According to Circular 22/89, paragraph 29, 'these procedures focus upon a group of children within the larger group of children with special educational needs'. In theory, a statement contains a legally binding record of the provision required to overcome the difficulties a child faces. Some people see the process of producing statements as a major step forward in ensuring that the difficulties of pupils are catered for appropriately and that their parents are involved in decisions taken about them. Parents must, for example, be given copies of all the advice that is used in determining the statement and have opportunities to comment on the statement in draft form and to appeal against its content where they disagree with it.

3.56 Statements are also seen as a financial safeguard, as being the only way that schools and local education authorities will give financial priority to those who need the additional support of staff and equipment. Others see them as an instrument of educational policy; they argue that a special education policy can be constructed piece by piece from decisions made about the individual needs of children and young people during the preparation of statements.

Statements in practice

3.57 Since the preparation of statements (or records in Scotland) is governed by the legal framework of the Education Act 1981, those involved in their preparation are pushed towards the way of viewing and talking about difficulties in learning contained in that document unless they have carefully worked out a view for themselves and then use the procedures strategically.

3.58 Statements can be written for a child from the age of birth to 19 years and a summary of the procedures are given opposite. Some of you may already be familiar with these procedures. As well as in the 1981 Act, they are set out in regulations issued in 1983 which have the force of law (Education (Special Educational Needs) Regulations 1983) and in a

> # Summary of procedures
>
> ### Children under two
> **Parent** can ask for *assessment*;
> **District Health Authority** must tell **parent**, then **education authority**, that child may have *special educational needs*;
> **Education authority** may with *consent* of **parent**, and *must at request* of **parent**, make an *assessment*. It can be of any kind, and may result in a *Statement of Special Educational Needs*.
>
> ### Children between two and 19
> **Authorities** have a *duty to identify* children *whose special educational needs* call on the **authority** to decide on *special educational provision*;
> **Parents** can request *assessment* and **authorities** cannot *unreasonably refuse*.
>
> ### *Assessment*
> *Notice* to **parents** — *29 days* to comment;
> If **authority** decides *not to assess*, must *notify* **parent**;
> **Parents** must receive *notices* of any *examinations*; have a right to be present and to submit information;
> **Parents** who fail to see that their children turn up for examinations without *reasonable excuse* may be *guilty* of offence and *fined*.
>
> ### After assessment
> **Authority** may decide *not to make Statement* of Special Educational Needs: must inform **parent** of *right of appeal* to **Secretary of State**;
> If **authority** decides to *make Statement*; must serve copy of *draft* statement on **parent**;
> If **parent** *disagrees* with any part:
>   *within 15 days* can make *representations*, ask for meeting with **officer**;
>   *within further 15 days*, ask for other *meetings* to discuss professional advice provided to authority (which must be given to parent as part of Statement);
>   *within final 15 days* from last meeting, make further *representations* to authority.
> **Authority**, after considering parents' views can make *Statement* in the same or changed form, or decide not to make it: must *inform* **parent**.
> If *Statement* is made, must be sent to **parent** with *notice of right to appeal* in writing to *local appeal committee*, which can *confirm Statement*, or ask authority to *reconsider* it;
> **Parent** has further *right of appeal* to **Secretary of State**.
>
> ### After Statement is made
> **Statements** must be *reviewed* within every 12 months;
> **Child** with *Statement* must be *re-assessed* between age of 12½ and 14½.
> **Parent** can *appeal* following any *re-assessment* or any *amendment* of a *Statement*.
> **Authority** must see that special educational provision set out in Statement is made.

(Advisory Centre for Education, 1990, p. 16)

circular (updated in 1989 and 1991 following the 1988 Education Act) which is advisory (Circular 22/89 and the draft addendum; DES, 1989a and 1991). In Appendix 2 I have included the documents which appear as annexes at the end of this circular. They consist of:

- a checklist on the advice that should be gathered in the preparation of a statement from parents, teachers, educational psychologists, doctors and other relevant professionals;

- the recommended form for the production of the statement;
- the list of matters on which LEAs need to provide information to parents of children categorized as having special educational needs.

Activity 9   Defining the subject

Read Annex 1, 'Advice on special educational needs: suggested checklist' in Appendix 2 . What picture would you gain of the child or young person who is the subject of the information that would be gathered here? Look at the areas of development that should be attended to under 'Aims of provision'. Does the breakdown of development into physical, motor, cognitive, language and social areas leave anything out? Would the resulting report describe a child or young person who sounds like anyone you know?

3.59   Circular 22/89, paragraph 17, tells us that 'the extent to which a learning difficulty hinders a child's development does not depend solely on the nature and severity of that difficulty' but also on a child's personal characteristics, the support at home and the provision already made for them. Paragraph 17 goes on to suggest that 'a child's special educational needs are thus related both to abilities and disabilities, and to the nature and extent of the interaction of these with his or her environment'. I believe there is a contradiction between these two suggestions. The first implies that learning difficulties are something *children* have, albeit they can be exacerbated by other factors. The second that learning difficulties (special needs, officially, are a kind of learning difficulty) are formed in a relationship between children and their setting. It is the first of these ideas which dominates the suggestions for the gathering of advice in preparing a statement.

3.60   The contradictory ideas in the circular are apparent again in paragraph 51:

> Advice should be relevant and usable in an educational context, and available to teachers to enable them to plan a detailed programme of education for the pupil. Advice should not be influenced by consideration of the eventual school placement to be made for the child, since that is a matter to be determined by the LEA at a later stage.

The problem with these two sentences can be illustrated by Julia, a child in a primary school. She sits working at a table with a group of pupils. The task she has been given is to use a worksheet to answer questions about the bean she has grown on blotting paper. She cannot read the questions. The group round the table are not much help to her. They are the 'low attainers' group. A statement is to be produced about her. What are her educational needs?

3.61   Now, there are all sorts of positive suggestions that can be made about the way Julia might be helped to gain access to her science lesson;

about ways of recording her knowledge and observations; about grouping policies in her classroom; about the possibilities for co-operative learning; about the use that can be made of the support available in the school; about the sharing of teacher expertise within the school; about the expertise that can be drawn on from support services external to the school. But for the purposes of the statement advice must avoid discussing a particular school; Julia's school. Doesn't this limit the relevance and usefulness of the advice?

3.62 If it is unfamiliar to you, have a look at the proposed format for statements, also in Appendix 2 (Annex 2 of the original document). Part III indicates that, although they do not have to, statements may specify the way the National Curriculum can be modified for children as part of the 'special educational provision' that is made for them.

3.63 Despite the problems of procedure and definition and the difficulties of communication which can follow, such documents do sometimes contain careful considerations of the educational requirements of pupils which lead to constructive plans for their education. But statements may also be used cynically, without a serious attempt to understand the detailed requirements of particular pupils. Those who worked on the research project into the implementation of the 1981 Act commissioned by the Department of Education and Science concluded:

> The impression given by many of the statements we saw in the course of our research is that they were solely concerned with the relocation of children and that they were written from Part IV (the identification of the appropriate school) backwards. That is, the provision is decided, then the requisite formula is slotted into Part III (special educational provision) and Part II (special educational needs) to justify the placement.
> (Goacher et al., 1988, p. 115)

They found that statements were 'detailed ... if the particular needs of a child can be met in a mainstream setting ... whereas if the needs can be generally met within a certain type of provision, for example, a school for moderate learning difficulties, the needs and provision are formulated in a more general way. There is a tendency for statements of the latter kind to use certain stock phrases to describe needs and provision' (p. 114).

3.64 Much has been made of the provision for parental involvement in the writing of statements. As discussed in Unit 3/4, the 1981 Act prompted the emergence of a number of parent support groups, for example Network 81. Such groups generally emerged in order to encourage parents to assert their rights against perceived negative treatment from professionals and administrators. In the DES-commissioned research mentioned earlier, although 'not all parents' were said 'to have negative feelings about the identification and assessment process', many did. Typical comments were:

> If I knew what I knew now, I would have refused to take part in all those assessments and case conferences ... It was all so negative.

> We were not really informed enough. Each time we were given no option really, and it is difficult to decide if it is the right school if you are given the only one.
> (Goacher *et al.*, 1987, p. 127)

Many reports have emerged from parents and voluntary societies, documenting the poor treatment parents have received during the statementing process and their view of the frequently unsatisfactory nature of its outcomes (Cornwell, 1987; Greater London Association for Disabled People, 1988; Malek with Kerslake, 1989; NDCS, 1989; Stone, 1987).

Statements as policy

3.65 Statements are costly. There was information available at the time the 1981 Act was being formulated that the Individual Educational Plan (IEP) brought in by Public Law 92–142 in the United States, from which some of the ideas for statements were derived, was fraught with difficulties. Federal funds were made available for pupils on the completion of the assessment procedures leading up to the writing of the IEP. Thus the authorities in some school districts saw it as in their interests to produce as many IEPs as possible. This began to produce greater inequalities than already existed between school districts, since the wealthier areas had larger numbers of professionals to carry out assessments and gain extra funds. As far as the whole system was concerned, resources began to be poured into the assessment process, reducing their availability for educational provision. In the end a ceiling of 12 per cent was placed on the numbers of students that could have IEPs. It was clear, too, in the 1970s that IEPs did not live up to the claim that they gave parents the right to participate in assessment procedures. As in the statementing process, they provided a technical arena which was alien to most parents and was biased in favour of professional advisers.

3.66 It is hard to see how statements can be used as an equitable instrument of budgetary policy when they are used to such a different extent by different LEAs. The House of Commons Select Committee reported in 1987 that there was a 'wide variation between LEAs both in the percentage of pupils who are the subject of statements and in the percentage of children who are having their needs met in primary and secondary schools'. Despite this and other evidence, Circular 22/89 obscures this issue when it states: 'Since the implementation of the 1981 Act, attention has tended to focus on the 2 per cent of the school population who have statements ... ' (DES, 1989a, p. 6).

3.67 It may be that there is an intention here to regulate the numbers who are statemented. But what would be the consequences of knowing in advance that there were to be 2 per cent of pupils who would be the subject of statements? It then becomes possible to allocate resources based on presumed need without recourse to the statementing process. If 2 per cent of the school population are staffed with a pupil–teacher ratio of six to one, say, then the statementing process need only be invoked when there is dispute over whether the needs of particular pupils are being recognized. Rather than being seen as an instrument of policy, statements might have a role only when policies have broken down.

3.68 Local management of schools (LMS), introduced in 1990 following the Education Act 1988, is shifting responsibility onto schools to control their own budgets, but LEAs still retain extensive powers of inspection to determine that priority is given to supporting and reducing difficulties in learning. These issues are discussed, along with appeals procedures, in Unit 15.

Activity 10 Ruled out or rescued?

'Ruled out or rescued? A statement for Balbinder' is an account of the statementing of Balbinder, a boy in his second year of infants' school who was felt by his teachers to be making slow progress. It illustrates the decisions and choices that are made for pupils and raises questions about the nature of possible support in mainstream schools, particularly for pupils whose first language is not English. It is written by Elizabeth Grugeon, a friend of Balbinder's family, and is an edited version of a chapter in *Educating All* (Grugeon and Woods, 1990). We have included it as Chapter 15 in Reader 2.

I suggest that you read through the account quickly, and then go back over it considering the following questions:

- What do you feel the experience of attending the playgroup was like for Balbinder?
- What could have been done to facilitate better contact between the school and Balbinder's family?
- What image do you get of the curriculum that Balbinder is expected to follow in his old and new schools? How is it described by the headteachers?
- What aspirations does his mother have for him?
- What approach does the psychologist take to assessment?
- To what extent do 'social' and 'behavioural concerns' affect the decision of his primary school to recommend transfer?
- What do you see as the pros and cons of Balbinder's transfer to special school? What are the advantages and disadvantages which are discussed with Balbinder's parents (and Balbinder)?
- To what extent does the statementing process reflect an open and imaginative exploration of the best way to support Balbinder's education?
- To what extent are Balbinder's 'educational needs' assessed separately from the provision and place where these needs might be met?

- What pictures do you get of Balbinder's wishes? How involved do you feel he should be in decisions that are taken about him?

- What do you see as the significance of Balbinder's and his mother's concern about other pupils with an Asian background at the school?

- What do you learn about the particular needs of pupils whose first language is not English?

3.69   At the end of the version of Balbinder's story in *Educating All*, Elizabeth Grugeon added the following postscript:

> Too late for Balbinder, the Report of the Task Group on Assessment and Testing recognized that 'there may be difficulties presented by those whose first language is not English' and felt that to record a low level of performance for this reason would not reflect a pupil's general ability. Furthermore, it recommended that 'assessment in other skills and understanding, particularly at age seven, should, wherever practicable, be conducted in the pupil's first language' ... However, at the time that Balbinder was demonstrating his newly acquired confidence and his developing communicative competence, the conference, 'Asian Children and Special Education', was discussing issues of importance both to him and other Asian children involved in special education: home–school relations; mother-tongue information to parents; parental rights and the need for independent interpreters. The recommendations that arose from this conference, for strengthening support and appropriate provision for Asian children with special needs, seem a fitting postscript to the story of Balbinder:
>
> - to urge that every education authority with ethnic minority communities employ a number of bilingual liaison officers to inform and communicate with parents;
>
> - to urge education authorities to provide information in mother-tongue languages;
>
> - to ensure that information, especially legal documents, be delivered by hand by someone capable of speaking the family's first language and of explaining the meaning of the document;
>
> - to encourage the use of a pool of teachers in each school which have linguistic backgrounds who can liaise with parents and maintain community languages in schools;
>
> - to urge schools to communicate to parents using trained interpreters where necessary, before a crisis occurs, in an attempt to remedy minor problems at an early age;
>
> - to highlight the need for more research to be done on unbiased psychological tests for children; there was acknowledgement that while present tests are culturally biased, there remains a need for some objective measures to identify a child's particular needs;

- to encourage the use of bilingual professionals and the use of the child's first language in assessments;
- to urge education authorities to support independent advice centres, similar to the ACE project, in each city. (ACE, 1989, pp. 3–4)

(Grugeon and Woods, 1990, pp. 84–5)

3.70 Circular 22/89 provides clear guidelines for the assessment of children who, like Balbinder, speak a language at home other than English:

> In assessing the child's special educational needs, it is important to take account of the possibility that cultural differences may mask the child's true learning potential or indeed the nature and extent of his or her special needs. Authorities should ensure that the language in which notices are served on the child's parent is one with which the parent will be familiar or, failing that, a language for which he or she can readily obtain an interpreter. LEAs may find it helpful to make special arrangements to bring in a person with knowledge of the language and cultural background of the child and the parent in the various stages of assessment.
>
> (DES, 1989a, p. 26)

3.71 The staff in many schools have considered and implemented effective ways of supporting their bilingual pupils. At Edgehill Primary School in Coventry, for example, the staff rethought their concepts of learning support so that they included the difficulties faced by pupils acquiring English as a second language (Bailey and Skoro, 1987).

A persistent culture of assessment and placement

3.72 My own interest in the assessment process dates from 1970 when as a newly qualified educational psychologist I found myself faced with the task of persuading parents to accept the placement of their children in special schools. By and large they did not think it was a very good idea and by and large I managed to gain their acceptance in the end. However, I soon began to question my own faith in the correctness of my decisions. What gave me the idea that my judgement of what was in the interests of these young people was better than that of their own parents? Who was more likely to have the interests of these pupils at heart? I realized that my ready patter had been passed on and accepted uncritically during my educational psychology training and that I had been simply unaware of alternative views about the purpose and effects of segregation. It was at a time when a furore was beginning to surface about the over-representation of black pupils in ESN(M) schools. I had a look at what happened to black pupils where I worked and gained a number of insights. First, there was an over-representation of black pupils in my area too, and secondly, I could not get any of my educational psychologist colleagues to take any interest in the matter. They felt that each case was decided on its merits and that special schools provided a form of positive discrimination. They simply would not believe that black parents objected to the presence of their children there. By taking each case on its merits, one could not be aware of the subtle processes of racism which might lead one to tip the balance of a decision at each stage of the assessment process. The way in which this happens has been carefully documented since, both in the US and the UK (Mercer, 1973; Tomlinson, 1981).

3.73 I came to realize that if I was to make intelligent decisions about my own working practices I had to be aware of their political and historical context. I was somewhat startled to discover the advice Binet and Simon, early developers of intelligence testing, gave to those charged with placing pupils in special schools. Written in 1914, it closely parallels the arguments I thought were my own:

> When legislation provides special schools and classes for the benefit of defectives, it will be imprudent to make use of legal force to bear down the will of the parents. It will be better, in the first instance, to have recourse to persuasion. It will be pointed out to the parents that their children are behind hand in their own lessons ... It will be explained to them that classes of forty pupils are too large for children like theirs, and that the teacher cannot devote sufficient attention to them. It will be explained also that classes are being organized for ten to twenty pupils at most, in which it will be possible to give individual attention ... One will appeal to the heart of their parents, and will surely manage to persuade them, especially the mothers ... It would never do to say to the parents that their child is an idiot, an imbecile, a fool or even abnormal. The admission of their son or daughter into a special school should be represented to them as an advantage or even a favour.
> (Binet and Simon, 1914, p. 36)

Do you find echoes of these sentiments in the case study of Balbinder?

3.74 Binet and Simon were asking here for parents to be deceived by professionals about the true purpose of special schooling. The presence of 'retarded' pupils in state schools was seen by them as a threat to social stability and professionals were being asked to act in the 'social interest'. The authors were aware too how easy it might be for other interests to be served by the emerging special schools:

> Ever since public interest has been aroused in the question of schools for defective children, selfish ambition has seen its opportunity. The most frankly selfish interests conceal themselves behind the mask of philanthropy, and whoever dreams of finding a fine situation for himself in the new schools never speaks of children without tears in his eyes. This is the everlasting human comedy. There is no reason for indignation. Everyone has the right to look after his own interests, so long as he does not compromise interests superior to his own ...
> (Binet and Simon, 1914, p. 10)

3.75 Now I do not think that most people who work within special schools defend their existence through self-interest, though some do. I have watched with some amusement how some advocates of integrated provision have become staunch supporters of segregation when they have applied for and been appointed to a position as head of a special school. However, I have also been impressed by the imaginative schemes, devised by the heads and staff of special schools, for moving pupils into the mainstream and supporting them there. Sometimes these efforts have foundered on the inadequacies of the administrative machinery for transferring resources in the LEA and on the deficiencies in plans for allocating money under LMS. In contrast, Chapters 4 and 5 in Reader 2 both describe the successful efforts of the staff of special schools to transform their schools. These chapters will be discussed in Unit 16.

Where do they go?

3.76 What happens to children who are the subject of statements? Are they, like Balbinder, directed towards special schools? Once a special school is recommended in a statement, parents are legally obliged to send their child there unless they win an appeal against the statement's contents. You may believe that a special school is the right place for the education of some children. Do you also think that some parents should be *compelled* to send their children to special schools? Circular 22/89 refers to the fact that 'the 1981 Act placed LEAs under a duty to secure that, subject to conditions specified in Section 2(3), children with statements should be educated in ordinary schools' (paragraph 22). When the 1981 Act emerged there was considerable debate about precisely what its so-called integration clause implied. The conditions of Section 2(3) are that:

> account has been taken ... of the views of the child's parent and that educating the child in an ordinary school is compatible with –
>
> (a) his receiving the special education provision that he requires;
>
> (b) the provision of efficient education for the children with whom he will be educated; and
>
> (c) the efficient use of resources.
>
> (Education Act 1981, Section 2(3))

Some people saw these exceptions as permitting an expansion in the special school population, while others argued that since these conditions were satisfied somewhere for children irrespective of the severity of their difficulties or disabilities, then they could be satisfied for almost all children everywhere. I argued that, for it to have any legal meaning, the phrase 'provided it is compatible with' should be taken to mean 'provided it can be made compatible with'. This would tip the balance of Section 2 firmly in favour of integration. In the event, the years after the implementation date of the Act on 1 April 1983 have seen a small initial rise, then a small gradual drop in the special school population. According to the figures available for 1990, there were 97,000 pupils attending special schools, representing 1.34 per cent of the school population, and a further 54,000 students who had statements in the mainstream. Of these, 36,000 were on the register of mainstream classes while 18,000 were on the register of special classes or units.

3.77 Despite the advice of Circular 22/89, it is not the norm for pupils with statements to be educated in the mainstream, though 1990 was the first year during which there were almost the same number of new statements recommending mainstream places as there were special school places. Whether or not this trend continues may depend on how the 1988 Act is interpreted within schools. Will the Act encourage mainstream schools to be less tolerant to a diversity of pupils?

Assigning a category

3.78 After the implementation of the 1981 Education Act in 1983 the DES stopped publishing information on the way students and special schools were categorized. However, this does not mean that pupils are no longer considered in that way. Based on the 1983 statistics, about half of the pupils in special schools are categorized as having 'moderate learning difficulties' and a quarter as having 'severe learning difficulties'. The next most popular category is 'emotional and behavioural difficulty' and then 'physical disability', with smaller numbers attending schools for deaf students or pupils with visual disabilities. The changes in the special school population have been so slow that these proportions are still generally the same, though practice varies from authority to authority.

3.79 While in education categorization according to ability and disability has been replaced in official documents by the language of 'special needs' and 'learning difficulty', the Children Act 1989 framed by the Department of Health, which was implemented in October 1991, reintroduced into law an obligation for local authorities to categorize by and collect statistics on disability in children and young people. The Act introduced the notion of 'children in need' to cover children who need the support of social services to maintain 'a reasonable standard of health or development' or to stop impairment to 'health or development' or if they are 'disabled'.

3.80 For its definition of disability the Children Act harks back to the National Assistance Act of 1948. A child is said to be 'disabled' in the Act 'if he is blind, deaf or dumb or suffers from mental disorder of any kind or is substantially and permanently handicapped by illness, injury or congenital deformity or such other disability as may be prescribed' (Children Act 1989, Section 17 (11)). Why would those writing an Act in 1989 wish to define disability in such antiquated terms? Why would they reproduce an ancient characterization of deaf people as having no voice; of being dumb? Such definitions reinforce the message of this section, unit and course that you have to decide for yourself the best way to think about difficulties in learning, disability and approaches to teaching and learning.

SUMMARY

3.81 This section has covered a vast amount of ground. It started with the question, 'Who experiences difficulties in school?' and I suggested that the answer includes a wider group than those who experience difficulties in learning. The nature of the difficulties brought to our attention depends on who identifies them and the point of view from which they are described. Priorities change too, because problems change or because our awareness and concern about them alters. I suggested a number of difficulties that we might recognize as affecting students in school and looked in particular detail at children and young people affected by HIV and AIDS, children in care and traveller children – the last as an example of a group who have to face discrimination inside and outside schools. The extent to which we recognize and act on a particular problem has implications for the resources that remain to tackle other issues.

3.82 I then moved on to the question, 'When and why is learning difficult?' and argued that it made little sense to think of difficulties in learning as the province of a small group of students who are relatively low in attainment. I used the example of a science lesson to indicate the way any group of students can have difficulties in learning if they are unable to fully understand what they are expected to learn. I then considered the way official documents have pushed us to think of the difficulties of students as confined to a group having 'special needs' or 'learning difficulties'. I called into question the sense of estimating the numbers in such categories and took you through the definitions in the 1981 Education Act. I urged you to avoid gobbledegook by thinking out your own definitions of learning difficulties and special needs.

3.83 Children and young people may be made the subject of statements because they experience difficulties in learning but it may be that they have a physical disability that requires adaptations to be made to a school building. I provided details of the statementing procedures and discussed their usefulness in ensuring that students have appropriate curricula and that LEAs develop appropriate policies. Whatever other effects statements may have, one outcome for most pupils who are their subject is that, for them, attendance at a special school is compulsory. You will have to assess the extent to which this is true in your area and remains true nationally.

4 SCHOOLS, PUPILS AND CURRICULA

4.1 How should schools be organized so that difficulties in learning are minimized? How should they respond to the diversity of their students? How should curricula be presented? In this section I will introduce you to some of the ways in which teachers have attempted to answer these questions. I will concentrate in particular on two schools, the Grove Primary School in Cambridge and Whitmore High School in Harrow. Both these schools also include young people with disabilities. Many of the issues I will raise will be looked at in greater detail in Units 6/7 and 8/9, though we do not present a single shared view among the different unit authors, nor, I suspect, do we offer arguments free of contradictions as individuals.

4.2 To what extent should we place different pupils on different curriculum tracks? Bernard Fairhurst teaches environmental science in Gloucestershire. Like teachers in the Grove and Whitmore schools, he argues that shared experiences in mixed groups can form the basis for differentiated teaching and learning. He is aware, however, that his own subject has been seen at times as near the bottom of a status hierarchy of science teaching:

> I had an interview in a secondary school for a post in a science department where the curriculum was described as 'normal sciences for the able pupils, general science for the less able, environmental studies for the still weaker pupils and horticulture for the really low ability'. I described this as an attitude of 'vegetables for vegetables' and did not get the job.

4.3 As part of his plan to involve the school and its community in environmental science he is developing a mixed-habitat area:

> I was able to get support and guidance from the horticultural adviser, a grant from the Nature Conservancy Council and design work and labouring by the pupils. Initial stages involved showing students the bit of school field, identifying the range of plants present and discussing how variety could be increased. Then drawing scale plans with the pupils designing a mixed-habitat area with all possible inclusions coming from them, e.g. pond, marsh, grassland, shrubs. As well as looking at the area, I prompted them with questions, e.g., 'How would you encourage amphibians? … reptiles? … flying mammals? … hedgehogs? … butterflies?' These provoked further thoughts and additions to plans. The questions, 'What about access for people in wheelchairs? Or plants for people who are visually impaired?' provoked various responses from interest and appreciating the need to rethink access, pathways, height of beds, varieties etc., to, 'What has that got to do with a habitat area?' or 'What has that got to do with our school?' We discussed the role of the school in providing a service to all the community. Students begin to see that in a small area a large range of plants and animals can be encouraged through careful management and gain an insight into ecological relationships. Feeders and bird and bat boxes could be built, flowers and shrubs planted for scent and nectar …
>
> (personal communication)

4.4 Environmental science, besides providing an infinite variety of fruitful shared experiences for students, is also a fertile source of metaphors for education and society. For some, competition for ecological niches and a struggle for survival may seem suitable models for the classroom environment. However, the metaphors that you choose depend on your ideological preconceptions. The creation of a mixed habitat in which a diversity of plants and animals flourish may require careful, planned and repeated intervention.

UNDER THE WALNUT TREE: THE GROVE PRIMARY SCHOOL

4.5   The first television programme for this course is called *Under the Walnut Tree* (the tree is to be found in the central courtyard of the school) and is a documentary about the Grove Primary School in Cambridge. It portrays the past and present, the curriculum and organization of the primary school. To support and extend the film, I have written a detailed account of the school which is Chapter 1 in Reader 2. I hope you will read this account *after* you have watched the programme to maximize its dramatic impact. I have used many of the interviews gathered in

constructing the programme in the preparation of the account. The written account of the Grove story should help you consider and react to the issues that are raised, but the written document does not replace the film and you are strongly urged to watch the programme. This course is partly about examining and criticizing educational television; about exploring the impact of the images and arguments it contains.

4.6   In Thomas Hardy's novel, *Under the Greenwood Tree*, the tree bears witness to the passing generations in a manner reminiscent of the opening of a book for children. It has relevance, therefore, for a story about a primary school:

> Many hundreds of birds had been born amidst the boughs of this single tree; tribes of rabbits and hares had nibbled at its bark from year to year; quaint tufts of fungi had sprung from the cavities of its forks; and countless families of earthworms had crept about its roots. Beneath and beyond its shade spread a carefully-tended grass-plot, its purpose being to supply a healthy exercise-ground for young chickens and pheasants.
>
> (Hardy, 1872; p. 205 of the paperback edition)

4.7   I thought I was making a reference to Hardy in my title for the television programme and chapter but I should have realized that the archaeological imperative, that turning over a stone always reveals something underneath, applies here too. Hardy, too was making a reference, not, as the introduction to my edition of *Under the Greenwood Tree* tells me in my ignorance, to *As You Like It*, but to a sixteenth- or seventeenth-century ballad, 'describing rustic merrymaking':

> O how they firk it, caper and jerk it
> Under the greenwood tree

I leave you to decide for yourselves on the appropriateness to education of the resonances of this refrain.

Activity 11   Pictures from the Grove

I hope that you can arrange your study of this unit so that you can watch TV1, *Under the Walnut Tree*, at this point. If at all possible I suggest you watch it with other course members so that you can pool your reactions. If you have the opportunity to record the programme so that you can stop and start it on a second run through, so much the better. *Write down and, if possible, discuss your reactions to the programme.* What did it remind you about? Do not feel constrained, here, to stick to the themes of the programme but be aware when you are not. Watching a programme like this can be useful on more than one level. It may link into an element of your experience or ideas that it is useful to explore. Jot down these more tangential links first then concentrate more specifically on the programme's content. Did you learn anything from it? What would you like to know more about?

4.8   Did you resist learning from and about the subject matter of the programme? A council-built estate in Cambridge is not inner-city London or Glasgow or Belfast or Cardiff. It is not rural Yorkshire or Cornwall. It is one particular place and could not be anything else. We were not trying to pick an 'easy setting' to demonstrate the virtues of inclusive educational policies, nor to say that the way education has developed in this setting is the best it could have been. However, we have tried to explain something about why the school has developed in the way it has.

4.9   The making of the programme has its own story. I selected the Grove school because I thought it could be used to introduce many of the issues of the course. I also chose it because it is near my home and I want to encourage you to get to know and begin to study your own areas. It seems sensible to make this a shared task. My first ideas were for a more ambitious programme about the various communities connected to the Grove; of pupils, school workers, parents and in the surrounding estate. I wanted, too, to examine the pressure on schools to become suppliers of attractive commodities, in competition with others for the patronage of their customers, rather than an integral part of the life of the surrounding community. I realized, however, that this would require a series to itself, rather than a single 25-minute programme.

4.10   The issues concerning a school and its communities are alluded to but are not now central to the programme and the written account. Nevertheless the scaled-down project, of giving some idea of the functioning of the school, is still large enough to mean that issues can only be introduced rather than examined in depth.

4.11   If you feel frustrated by the lack of information on a certain issue, put yourself in our position as programme makers and consider what you would have left out. Perhaps you would have limited yourself to a single issue from the start. But the task of portraying a primary school in which some of the pupils have disabilities would have suffered if the curriculum or classroom organization, the ordinariness of life, were omitted. Nor is there a great deal of detail about the disabilities of the pupils in the programme. While we were making the film it was hard not to see the pupils as part of the audience for it. We wished to avoid talking about any of the pupils as if they were objects of study. But perhaps, anyway, you will feel that the pupils with disabilities receive too much attention in the film.

4.12   When you take a camera crew into a school where there are children with disabilities there is a tendency for the crew to assume that the film will be about disability; for the camera to linger on a child with disabilities rather than the learning of another class member. We tried to minimize the effects of this tendency during the shooting and editing of the film. Did we succeed?

Activity 12   Responding to images

What does this photograph tell you?

What are your reactions to it?

What does it convey about pupils with disabilities?

One person observing the photograph asked why the boy in the wheelchair was stuck out on the left.

Look at the direction of gaze of the girl to the right of centre.

How do you react to these remarks?

4.13   Before the start of filming we decided that we would have no face-to-face camera interviews. This was partly because we wanted to try something different from other programmes we had made in the past but also to make the images give a more active and realistic portrayal of the school. None of the schoolworkers spend their day sitting around giving television interviews. We used photographs to extend the range of settings from those that our budget allowed, to permit discussion of the school's history and because we liked them.

4.14   I suspect that your viewing of the programme will leave many loose ends. What does a particular worker do? What difficulties does a particular pupil experience? What did the pupils learn on the trip? It is in an attempt to further unravel *some* of these leads that I have produced a written account to support the film.

Activity 13 The book of the film

Now read 'Under the walnut tree: the Grove Primary School', Chapter 1 in Reader 2. As you go through it write down the questions it raises for you. What does it add to the programme? What is still omitted? Near the beginning I set out three aims: to portray a school, pupils and staff that have a past and a future; to sample the curriculum; and to examine the way pupils with disabilities are included within the school. Are these aims adequate? Are they fulfilled?

4.15 The chapter I have written about the Grove is quite long, yet it only scratches the surface of the life of the school and takes up only a small number of the issues which were raised by my observations. I will take some of them a little further here but most matters will have been given more thorough attention by the end of the course. I made the point at the start of the chapter that investigations in one school can be seen to interconnect with most contemporary and historical issues in education.

Activity 14 What would you choose to study next?

Make a list of those aspects of education raised by my account of the Grove school that you might wish to find out more about. What, if anything, captured your interest?

My own list, which reflects my own particular interests, may bear little resemblance to yours. It would include:

- the history of open-air schools (see below);
- the position and training of learning support assistants (these are called welfare assistants in TV1 and the reader chapter but see their new job title as more accurately reflecting their activities);
- the national trends in the education of pupils with physical disabilities and visual disabilities;
- the use of microtechnology with pupils with disabilities;
- the integration of pupils at secondary schools;
- techniques of physiotherapy, including conductive education;
- inconsistency in LEA policies;
- speech therapy, which is not discussed in my account;
- curriculum approaches across the school;
- approaches to gender and class;
- attitudes to ability;
- the multicultural content of the curriculum.

Scenes from the Grove: friendship, food, concentration, visits, community ...

Scenes from the Grove: support, working together, play, serious work.

Roger Ascham, a special school for children with physical disabilities, now closed. Originally its pavilions were built to provide an open-air education for pupils said to be 'delicate' in health or 'backward' in ability.

Activity 15 An open-air school

Appendix 3 is a description of the Roger Ascham school taken from *The Cambridge Chronicle and University Journal* for 1930. I obtained it from the local history collection at the central library in Cambridge. It describes the school a few years after it first opened and is included here to indicate a start that could be made to a local historical study. As you read it, consider how you might begin a historical project in your local area. What would you like to find out about? Who might you interview?

Curriculum and classroom support

4.16 The portrait of the curriculum of the Grove school which I included in my chapter is very selective indeed. There are thirteen class teachers in the school and I only included three of them. In TV1, besides the rat,

61

rocks and fen-life, there are two further lessons, a pottery lesson and a music and singing lesson. We did not suggest to teachers what should be shown on screen but we discussed what lessons were being considered and selected from them. So to some extent the principles underlying the lessons are a reflection of ideas I wanted to see portrayed in TV1, giving some indication of how common starting points might be taken in a number of different directions and to different levels depending on the interests and current competence of pupils. This is an important aspect of the teaching of a common curriculum to mixed groups.

4.17   How, for example, would you develop the ideas brought into the classroom with Tim Lister's fossil collection? Could you think of activities for pupils with a range of competencies? Having pupils engaged in a range of activities means that they will follow different paths in their learning. How important do you think it is to check on what pupils have gained through such experiences? Or are the energies of teachers better directed towards creating a classroom in which pupils are comfortable to learn rather than in the assessment of individual learning? When can we trust pupils to learn? How important are assessments in determining what should be taught next?

4.18   I do not know what proportion of lessons at the Grove are built around the direct experience of pupils, though it might be interesting to find out. How might this be done? One possibility would be to ask teachers to make brief daily notes on classroom activities over a week. Would this work? It might be better, though more time-consuming, to spend a day in each of a couple of classrooms to begin to see how activities might be classified. Or perhaps a discussion with a small group of teachers would reveal the best way to attempt it. If you are a primary school teacher, you will have a head start on designing such an activity.

Responsibility for the curriculum

4.19   In the Grove it is clear that the class teacher has overall responsibility for the curriculum. Sometimes, though not always, the support teachers do not know what is going to be happening before they arrive in the room. In other schools such as Whitmore, described below, there may be a greater emphasis on joint planning. Could the learning support assistants be involved in this planning exercise too?

Supporting pupils' learning

4.20   The pupils at the Grove are all members of mainstream classes, though, as the account makes clear, when the pupils with visual disabilities were first part of the school, they spent most of their time in their own room; they were a 'unit'. In other schools pupils may still be educated in this way. At Impington Village College, where pupils with physical disabilities transfer at eleven, more of the time, for several of the pupils, is spent in the purpose-built 'pavilion'.

4.21   At some schools, too, the provision for supporting pupils with disabilities is thought of as separate from the support for other pupils who may experience difficulties in learning. This is not so at the Grove. All pupils who experience difficulties are helped within the same support network. The changes that have taken place in such practices more generally, mirror the developments at the Grove. Withdrawal teaching has decreased and has been replaced by support in the classroom, though this has not been universally applied nor embraced without regret by all the staff in the schools in which it has occurred. Under either system the support available is often inadequate and there may be new pressures to reduce support as a result of LMS. The practice of learning support will be explored further in the discussion of Whitmore High School and in Unit 6/7.

Staffing levels

4.22   I mentioned in the account that the number of learning support assistants in the school is above the national norm for the support of pupils with disabilities in the mainstream. It is not above the numbers available in the nearby special schools. Could there be such a thing as optimum staffing levels? Could a school go on increasing the adult–pupil ratio indefinitely? Thelma's lesson contained four adults all busily supporting the pupils. If such numbers were available could they be profitably occupied in all lessons?

4.23   The staff are aware of the dangers of creating dependence and of getting in the way of pupils' independence, co-operative learning and social relationships. Can pupils negotiate the level of support they should receive? The need for support differs from pupil to pupil but in general one might suppose that the older the pupils the more sensitive one has to be about their privacy.

4.24   The job of a learning support assistant is a complex one but is not highly paid. After I completed the chapter for the reader, it transpired that the learning support assistants at the Grove were not after all going to be given parity with their colleagues in special schools. The LEA had entered into an agreement with the union that the special school learning support assistants were to be paid £600 per year more. This must make arguments about the transfer of pupils and resources from special schools into the mainstream more fraught as well as undermining an already vulnerable group of staff. In 1991 the county council started looking at the savings that could be made by reducing the support provided to pupils with disabilities in the mainstream. Grove school was told that they would have only seven instead of fourteen learning support assistants. Eventually the teachers and governors won the argument to retain their previous staffing levels.

POLICIES TOWARDS CHILDREN WITH DISABILITIES

4.25 What did you feel about the nature of the policy process portrayed in TV1 and Chapter 1 of Reader 2? There was some degree of planning but much depended on circumstance and fortune. The shaping of educational policy by fire is unlikely to be adopted generally. The way the Grove has developed is only one of many possibilities. You may question the concentration of pupils with disabilities in a single school. Could more be done to support pupils with disabilities so that they could attend their local schools? Does the school act like a magnet, drawing resources and expertise away from these communities? What are the advantages of the centralizing of resources at the Grove? How could the resources be distributed differently between the Grove and local schools?

4.26 There are two special schools in the vicinity of the Grove. One caters for pupils said to have 'severe learning difficulties', the other for pupils categorized as having 'moderate learning difficulties'. Is there something in the nature of these pupils that prevents their inclusion in mainstream schools? My view is that there is not, and that the particular group of pupils that is included from special schools depends on chance factors and the preconceptions and misconceptions of those with the power to initiate policy changes. I have two sorts of reasons for thinking this. One set refers to my experience. I have seen pupils incorporated effectively within mainstream primary and secondary schools irrespective of the severity of their disability or the difficulties they have with learning. The other set is conceptual. The most common arguments in favour of special schools are really arguments for centralizing of resources and, as the Grove illustrates, resources can be centralized within a mainstream school. The only legitimate arguments for segregation are those for isolation: that there is a group of pupils who need to be isolated from the mainstream either because this is a precondition for their education or because it is necessary for their protection or for the protection of others. How do these arguments strike you? Whom do you think should be excluded from the mainstream? Remember that when parents attempt to cushion their children from the hard edges of life they get called overprotective.

4.27 Some LEAs have made a more co-ordinated effort to effect changes in their schools than others. Most build their provision up in piecemeal fashion depending on the particular interests of education officers and local councillors, as well as the pressures from the schools, parents and central government. Why do you think LEAs have found large-scale planning so difficult? The 1988 Education Reform Act has provided LEAs, finally, with an excuse for lack of clarity of policy since it severely curtails their powers. Unit 15 explores the legitimacy of such an excuse.

Taking the support to pupils?

4.28 The Grove and Whitmore (described below) both provide an alternative to the segregation of pupils with disabilities in day or residential special schools. This particular alternative involves the centralizing of pupils and resources within particular mainstream schools. As was made clear in the discussion of the Grove school, this still separates some young people from their communities and can create difficulties at secondary transfer when attendance at the resourced school may involve new separation from friends and an absence of choice for pupils and parents.

4.29 Because it may not be at a local school, some people regard the attendance of a pupil at a resourced school as 'not proper integration', and as therefore not an improvement on attendance at a special school. It can be helpful to think of integration as *a process* of increasing the participation of children and young people within the mainstream. As a process it is never-ending. It can be applied to any pupil who is not a full participant in the core activities of mainstream schools, though what counts as central to the life of a school can be altered with greater ease than the interests and competencies of some pupils.

4.30 The planning of support for integrating special education provision within a LEA is affected by its geography. From the point of view of the planners it may seem sensible to centralize resources within urban centres. However, to parents or pupils in villages in rural authorities, daily travel to and from the nearest town may be unacceptable.

Activity 16 An achievement to be proud of

In Reader 1, Chapter 12, Alyson Clare has described the progress made by Chris Raine at the village school in Ravenstonedale in the Lake District, where she is the headteacher. Chris has Down's syndrome and initially, it had been decided, within his local authority, that he should attend a special school twenty miles from his home. Some people have an automatic response to children with Down's syndrome, that they all have severe learning difficulties and that they should all be in special schools. Alyson Clare offers us the opportunity to examine these assumptions and they will be further challenged in Unit 3/4.

Read Chapter 12 of Reader 1 now and, as you read, consider whether the description of Chris matches your expectations of children with Down's syndrome. Consider too the adaptations that are made by teachers and pupils. Do they go beyond the call of duty? Should the way they adapt to Chris's needs be unexceptional in schools? Alyson Clare argued for a *full-time* welfare assistant to support Chris's education because he was still in nappies when he started school. Is this a reasonable demand?

4.31 I know little about *your* expectations. However, I have met people, including some professionals, who find it difficult to accept that children with Down's syndrome may have developed powers of concentration and have an interest in books and reading. People with the syndrome are very varied in their interests and abilities. Some have profound and multiple disabilities. Others are capable, like Chris, of making considerable educational progress.

4.32 In the late 1970s I was involved with a group of parents who wanted to obtain a mainstream education for their children with Down's syndrome. Whenever I visit Cambridge University Library I am reminded of the low expectations some in the local authority held out for 'William' who was one of those children (Booth and Statham, 1982). He is now in his twenties and works in the library tea-room.

4.33 *The World of Nigel Hunt* is a book written about his travels and experiences by a young man with Down's syndrome. (He had wanted to write about pop music but his father persuaded him not to.) Nigel Hunt started his book by describing an illicit trip to London to witness the trooping of the colour.

> At the information office I asked for one single to St James's Park. Then I asked a porteress on the platform to ring my mum and tell her not to worry because I had gone to St James's Park. Then I asked myself and said I had better get out at Victoria.
>
> I sauntered to the Royal Mews and asked where Buckingham Palace is and the man said 'just keep to the left and you will come to it'. I asked a policeman when the band will be along and he said, 'ten and a half minutes'. So I stood and waited for at least one and a half minutes. I heard a teriffic throb and my ears were lifted and with a biff biff bang the band came along, and when they turned the corner up came their oompahs and the miserable trombones and blowed in the middle of nowhere.
>
> (Hunt, 1966, pp. 39–40)

4.34 Alyson Clare and Chris's teacher show a knack for turning the support they offer Chris into an educational opportunity for other children. Thus the whole school join in the learning of Makaton, a signing vocabulary based on British Sign Language, as well as the finger-spelling of letters of the alphabet. In helping Chris to develop the structure of his utterances they are likely to increase their own knowledge of syntax. The attention to and tolerance towards the educational requirements of one individual form a model which could be applied to any child. Is such a concentration on Chris likely to diminish or enhance an ability in schoolworkers and pupils for meeting the educational needs of others?

SECONDARY TRANSFER

4.35 In my account of the Grove I discussed some of the implications of secondary transfer, particularly for children with disabilities. Several of the changes that have taken place at Whitmore High School (described below) depended on the recognition by staff there of the value of methods developed within primary schools for working with groups within classes. There are problems for many pupils at transfer to secondary school, even though most manage it without a great deal of stress. Lynda Measor and Peter Woods have tried to understand the process of transfer from the point of view of pupils in *Changing Schools* (Measor and Woods, 1984).

Impington Village College

4.36 Impington Village College was the culmination of Henry Morris's project for a network of village colleges in Cambridgeshire. He was Chief Education Officer of Cambridgeshire from 1922 to 1954 and set out his vision for rural education in a memorandum published by Cambridge University Press in 1925.

> The village college would change the whole face of the problem of rural education. As the community centre of the neighbourhood it would provide for the whole man [sic], and abolish the duality of education and ordinary life. It would not only be the training ground for the art of living, but the place in which life is lived, the environment of a genuine corporate life. The dismal dispute of vocational and non-vocational education would not arise in it. It would be a visible demonstration in stone of the continuity and never ceasingness of education. There would be no 'leaving school'! – the child would enter at three and leave the college only in extreme old age. (In all seriousness it might be said that the 'school leaving age' would be lifted to 90.) It would have the great virtue of being local so that it would enhance the quality of actual life as it is lived from day to day – the supreme object of education. It would not be divorced from the normal environment of those who would frequent it from day to day, or from that greater educational institution, the family. Has there ever been an educational institution that at one and the same time provided for the needs of the whole family and consolidated its life – its social, physical, intellectual and economic life? Our modern educational institutions provide only for units of the family, or separate the individual from the family by time and space so that they may educate it apart and under less natural conditions. The village college would lie athwart the daily lives of the community it served; and in it the conditions would be realized under which education would be not an escape from reality, but an enrichment and transformation of it. For education is committed to the view that the ideal order and the actual order can ultimately be made one.
>
> (Morris, 1925, p. 154)

4.37 The college at Impington, built on land donated by the Chivers family of Histon, was opened in September 1939. At the memorial service for Henry Morris at Sawston Village College in 1962, Mr Edwards, who had been a teacher at the school, recalled the school's opening 'in spite of our national predicament'. He called the college 'this fairyland of his [i.e. Henry Morris's] creation ... with its magnificent trees, and with its abundance of light':

Activities at Impington: pupils with disabilities are involved in a wide range of activities in mainstream classes. Shown here are English, textiles and science, as well as a view into a classroom in the 'Pavilion'.

I like to believe that for a moment, at any rate, the seriousness of God's face was broken with a smile because of the joy that was in the hearts and illuminated the faces of those who came to teach no less than those who came to learn ...

(Mr Edwards, 9 March 1962, quoted in Farnell, 1968)

4.38 Some Impington staff feared that students with disabilities would be unable to cope with the standard of work expected in secondary school and wanted to reintroduce selection for some pupils on the basis of their attainment. There were initial fears that Madeleine Norman might find it difficult to cope with the school despite her relatively high levels of achievement. There is a traditional reluctance on the part of some secondary teachers to accept the accuracy of primary school reports about pupils. Sometimes this can work in the pupil's favour when they discard an unwarranted reputation or are given a fresh start. At other times it can condemn them to work again through material they have already covered. In Madeleine's case, despite the careful liaison from the Grove school, there seemed to be a limited understanding of her skills with information technology for a while after she started Impington. She was made to use a concept keyboard which involved less sophisticated technology and language than she had used with her light-talker. Nevertheless, when Jonathan Croall visited Impington Village College for *The Times Educational Supplement* in May 1991, Madeleine featured as one of the successes of the school's integration policy.

> 'Disabled people can mix with anybody; it's the able-bodied who can't always manage it.' Ronald Hunt speaks from experience. His daughter Karen, now aged eighteen, has severe cerebral palsy and is in a wheelchair. Her words are hard to follow. She is in pain much of the time and needs painkillers to keep her going.
>
> Yet unlike many physically disabled youngsters of her age and condition, Karen is no longer in a special school. Since 1987 she has been learning alongside able-bodied classmates at Impington Village College in Cambridgeshire.
>
> Her father is delighted. 'She's become more outgoing, it's broadened her horizons,' he says. 'At her special school she only had other disabled students to talk to. At her Guides they just didn't want to know. But at the college she mixes with the able-bodied children, and seems to get on with them. It's made her want to be more independent.' ...
>
> When Karen was three, her parents were told that her mental age would never reach more than half her actual age. Before coming to Impington she could not write and had never done any art. Yet last year she achieved a B grade in GCSE art – and the exam board graded her without knowing she was disabled ...
>
> I watched a group of two dozen year 7 students doing a science experiment which involved pouring silver nitrate into salty and

distilled water. Among them was Madeleine Norman who, like Karen, has cerebral palsy and is in a wheelchair. Two able-bodied students were working alongside her. Madeleine observed closely what was going on, but was also involved with the experiment as part of the group. She was able to hold a test tube and to take off her mask at the end of the experiment. On the front of her wheelchair she had a 'communications board', which had printed on it a wide range of words and phrases she might want to use.

Her classmates are well aware both of her capabilities and limitations. Her teacher, Toni Woodcock, adds: 'Madeleine's very active and knows what's going on. The other kids are brilliant, they really share with her. But it's a delicate balance – between getting her involved, and allowing her to see things happening.'

Striking the right balance is also important in relation to attitudes. On a wall in the Pavilion, as part of a student project on cerebral palsy, I found the statement: 'If people want to understand me, the first thing they've got to do is forget about my disability and talk to me as a person. Then they'll realise I'm just like anyone else.' ...

One testing-ground for equality of treatment is discipline. Staff say they try to be even-handed in dealing with anti-social behaviour. 'The disabled students can be just as naughty and irritating as the others,' Sylvia West says, remembering an occasion when she had to cram several wheelchairs and occupants into her office for a reprimand. In most schools you hear the traditional 'No running!' call from teachers. At Impington you hear 'No wheelies!'

But do the students themselves feel they are treated equally? Lisa Garrett, a cheerful 15-year-old with a 'Kick Ass!' sticker on the arm

Madeleine in her science lesson.

of her wheelchair has no doubts: 'I don't feel any different from the others. Most students accept you: they're helpful, but they don't show they're treating you differently.'

Oliver Dann has rather more mixed feelings. A bright, fairly outspoken 13-year-old, he thinks the school is 'pretty good'. He likes mixing with able-bodied students – several are his friends – and going to normal lessons. 'But some of the first-years treat me as if I was an idiot or a bit thick, as if I wasn't normal. I'd like to change that attitude.'

The able-bodied students I spoke to seemed quite clear and unsentimental about the issue. Amongst a group of 14-year-olds, one boy said: 'You don't feel embarrassed now when you see disabled people in the streets.' Another boy agreed: 'It's not strange, it's normal – but we still think of them as disabled.' A third said he didn't often talk to the disabled students. When I asked why, he said he didn't know – 'you're asking me things that make me realise I haven't thought very deeply about it.' ...

(Jonathan Croall, *The Times Educational Supplement*, 31 May 1991)

Activity 17 Bob's story

In Section 3 you read a fictionalized account of Pilgrim Way school. The authors of that account included the perspective of Bob, a primary school teacher with responsibility for liaising with the secondary school about students whom he thinks may experience difficulties there. He arrives on the day Fred is suspended. I have included his story as Appendix 4. Read it and consider the stereotypes of primary and secondary schools that emerge. As you progress through the course you will have further opportunities to assess whether they are justified.

WHITMORE HIGH SCHOOL

4.39 The changes that have taken place at Whitmore High School, in Harrow, parallel the developments at the Grove in many respects. The teachers have devised a unified system to support the learning of all pupils. They have broadened their community to include students with disabilities. Perhaps they have gone further than the Grove school in making explicit the nature of the changes they want to see and the philosophy underlying them as well as in encouraging the whole school to adopt them. Primary teachers might argue that as secondary teachers they actually had further to go before they could claim to be making the curriculum responsive to individual students.

Activity 18 Wholesale changes

Chapter 2 of Reader 2 is called 'A curricular response to diversity at Whitmore High School'. It is written by Christine Gilbert, who was then the headteacher, and by Michael Hart, the head of learning support, now known as learning development. (I will say more about this change of name later.) Read the chapter up to the end of section 2 (pp. 38–44). These first two sections describe the way the whole school was involved in change, and the nature of the approach to learning support which they introduced. What barriers do you see to the involvement of a whole school in policy development? How do you react to the way learning support is organized in this school?

A whole-school response

4.40 For some of you, the idea of all the staff of a school pulling in the same direction may seem entirely alien. You may be more used to schools in which there are as many points of view as there are members of staff. At the Grove, Thelma Jopling divided the staff into the progressives, the traditionalists and those in between 'who sit in meetings and say little'. We are not given details of the struggles and arguments at Whitmore, though in a 1,000 pupil secondary school with a large staff there must have been some. Who wins such struggles depends on who has the power and who can muster the most support. Christine Gilbert implies that as head she was in a strong position to initiate changes but was also able to gain support for what she represented as positive changes because the school had a falling roll and was under threat of closure.

4.41 The authors make clear elsewhere in the book from which the chapter is taken (Gilbert and Hart, 1990) that they also had the support of the local authority through its 'learning support policy' issued in 1986 as well as from the local authority special needs advisers. The policy was opposed by a headteacher of one of the local special schools who 'mounted an energetic campaign against the policy document'. The LEA started to transfer money into the mainstream that had been used previously to pay for students with disabilities to attend residential special schools. The progress of this integration policy can be seen in Table 1. The figures show a large net movement from residential to mainstream provision with a slight drop in numbers at Harrow's special schools.

Table 1 School attendance of students with statements in Harrow (aged 2–19).

	March 1986	January 1987	September 1989
Borough special school	254	237	210
Borough mainstream school	83	92	216
Out borough special school (day)	109	104	77
Out borough special school (residential)	118	106	49

(Source: adapted from Gilbert and Hart, 1990, p. 108)

From remedial extraction to learning support

4.42 Some of you may work in schools where the approach to overcoming difficulties in learning differs from that at Whitmore. It might seem that a new orthodoxy is being proposed which ignores the benefits of your method of working. Some teachers are very wary of giving up what they see as the advantages of direct teaching of pupils who experience difficulties, away from the scene of their failure.

4.43 Hellen Matthews, then a principal teacher in a secondary school in Aberdeen, wrote a brief account of her reactions to policy changes in her region of Scotland which she called 'The place of withdrawal' (Matthews, 1987). She records how, following a period when withdrawal from lessons was to be avoided at all costs, she came to regard it as having a value for particular purposes. Here she describes the criteria for deciding and the circumstances in which she would consider withdrawing a pupil from the mainstream:

> Now, when we discuss 'withdrawal' within this region we are speaking about precisely which settings are most appropriate for support in class, either in a quiet area of the classroom or in another room. The decisions made should be common-sense ones, taking account of the following kinds of consideration.
>
> 1   How easily distracted is the pupil with the tasks in hand?
>
> 2   Will the dialogue which the pupil and I shall share interfere with other talk going on in the classroom? Will our work be distracting to the other teacher or the rest of the class, either because of conversations cutting across each other or because the rest of the class is working quietly?
>
> 3   Will being overheard possibly embarrass the pupil being helped?
>
> The fact that the pupil may for some reason (e.g. prolonged absence) be doing completely different work is not in itself a sufficient reason for removing to another room, and pressure to do this becomes less where teaching-styles permit group or individual learning.
>
> There is a further question of how to assess the pattern of withdrawal for pupils with severe learning difficulties as the 'Parents' Charter' in the 1981 Education (Scotland) Act brings increasing numbers of such children into mainstream schools.
>
> One would hope that that particular phase in the wake of the Region's 'no-withdrawal' policy when teachers confused concepts of 'withdrawal' and felt they could never take a child to another room even if that would have been the best setting has now passed, and that common sense prevails. After all, pupils are still withdrawn repeatedly for individual music lessons, for example – would anyone suggest that trumpet lessons should take place in class? ...

The following examples illustrate different ways of dealing with learning difficulties in my school.

1 I would not withdraw a child in S1/S2 science here, as I cannot imagine a reason for it. The apparatus, the individualized style of learning, where all children in the laboratory are doing different things anyway, and the privacy which this situation generates, all point to in-class tutorial work ...

2 With *Tour de France* I often withdraw that group of pupils who have made low scores on the current criterion-referenced assessment. The course allows for revision and reassessment and, since Tour de France is a largely oral/aural course, to conduct such revision within the classroom where other work is going on would simply subject all pupils and staff to auditory interference: a quiet, separate room is much more satisfactory for everyone.

3 If, following an assessment in mathematics, a number of pupils reveal difficulties (despite in-class support) in a particular topic through which they have just worked, I withdraw them as a group for reasons of economy. I even, if numbers are small, withdraw pupils with similar difficulties across two mathematics classes taking place simultaneously. Here the setting may be either another part of a large maths area or another room, depending on need for boards, equipment, and so on. Following the 'remedial' session, pupils return to their maths classes and continue with their work, which is in any case individualized. On a day-to-day basis, individual help within the class is also given. Two points should be noted. Both settings for help – in and out of the classroom, individually or with other pupils – are commonplace and there is no fixed pool of 'remedial' pupils. A very able pupil having difficulty may also receive my help: our system aims to offer maximum flexibility.

A common-sense approach to learning-support derives from basic considerations about what is the best working-environment for the pupil. An environment full of noise and distraction which requires a constant filtering of irrelevant information is not a good learning-environment for most people. In making decisions as teachers, we should give some thought to how we learn most effectively ourselves and seek to establish an environment of equal quality for our pupils.

(Matthews, 1987, pp. 194–6)

4.44 The changes in approaches to learning support in Aberdeen were supported by clear guidelines from the local authority and from Scottish HMI. National guidelines for training courses were established so that a switch in approach would be reinforced (see Unit 6/7 and Fordyce, 1987). However, as an evaluation study has reported, the advocated practices have been taken up to varying extents in schools:

Co-operative teaching between learning support staff and subject or classroom teachers was found to be common; extraction of pupils from mainstream classes was relatively rare in secondary schools, but practised widely in the primary sector.

(Allan, Brown and Munn, 1991, p. 92)

4.45   In many local authorities the provision of learning support is not based in particular schools but in a peripatetic 'support service for special educational needs'. How can support teachers be an integral part of developments within a school if they are based outside it? Her Majesty's Inspectorate published a report of a survey of such support services in 1989. They found that often these services did not work closely with schools to produce a coherent policy on difficulties in learning:

> The majority of new services are based on peripatetic teams already working for the LEA. These teams generally consisted of remedial teachers who had worked with schools towards particular goals, e.g. assisting pupils with reading problems ... Too often classroom teachers reported confusing or conflicting advice from different advisory groups, for example about oral work, the grouping of pupils and the adaptation of teaching methods ... the general picture was one of fragmentation, with advisory services lacking common objectives.
>
> (DES, 1989b, pp. 4–6)

4.46   Fred Sedgwick has written more bluntly about the difficulty of fitting in a visitor, who expects to tackle the learning difficulty of a pupil, into the unpredictable life of a school:

On the outside looking in ...

Sam, who is six, came to me in agony. He's had various kinds of pain in his life so far ...

Sam's agony today was a creamy spotty lump outside a lower tooth. Biting on his playtime apple had started it off, and for ten minutes his wailing was unrelenting. Then Sue, the secretary, calmed him down with building bricks and other interesting plastic things cadged from the nursery for just this sort of purpose. And no doubt the hurt went away as the pressure subsided.

I rang school health for advice. Our nurse and her superior (I use the fashionable line management term) were on courses, so I tried the local dental clinic, and wonderfully, Sam was one of their patients; even better, they would see him straightaway.

But while this was going on, the visiting special needs teacher had turned up. Distracted by the noise from his systematic search for specific learning difficulties attached, however tenuously, to immature humans, he had found Sam. Taken him on his knee. Comforted him. And this had brought the yelling on, with a new vigour.

As Sue forced Sam's coat on, the special needs teacher asked me which children I would like him to see. He meant, were there any possible dyslexics about the place, and I resisted saying 'Here's a special need – sort this one out'. I was putting on my jacket at this point. Sam, quietened again by Sue, was waiting placidly ...

Eventually Sam and I got out to my car. At the dentist's it appeared he'd missed his last appointment. An abscess was diagnosed, and he was given antibiotics. I had lunch with him back at school, to make sure he had something soft – mince – and we both showed off our stickers: 'Hip hip hooray, no more decay'. I usually promise myself a salad and end up with chips. That's what happened today. Nursery crisis, nursery food.

When I got back to the office, the special needs teacher was at my side again. 'What children do you want me to see?' He always treats me as if he were the only person in the school I have to deal with. And our poor relationship, which is at least half my fault, is more than a personal clash: it underlines the deep gap that exists in thinking about special needs provision. On the one side are the basic-skillers, still talking almost entirely about phonics. On the other, those who want to broaden the action visiting teachers might take to include the whole curriculum, not to mention needs that can be defined only in human, not educational terms.

The first kind still takes children from their friends, the second keeps them together. The first concentrates on a part of the curriculum that the teacher and the child both know he or she can't cope with; the second sees the child as entitled to the whole curriculum, whatever his or her ability.

One of the first kind commented in our staffroom recently: 'Of course the children were more interested in what was going on around them than in my sentences'. Jeanette, my teacher, said, 'he should make his bloody sentences more interesting then, shouldn't he?'

The basic-skillers ply their trade in opposition to what bits of human life might be going on. I wish they'd see the business of being human in some coherent way, instead of fragmented into tables and test results. As our one fussed about while we were looking after Sam, he reminded me of a man who called at a house: 'Can I see Mr. Brown?' 'I'm afraid,' says the solemn man inside the front door, 'Mr. Brown died this morning. I am his brother and this [a weeping women in the hallway] is his widow.' 'Oh,' says the caller. 'Did he say anything about a pot of paint?'

(Sedgewick, 1988, p. 21)

4.47 We will return to the value and future of support services in Unit 15. In the financial circumstances of the early 1990s they appear to be under threat. Throughout the 1980s many teachers witnessed the cutting back of support staff (Gipps, Gross and Goldstein, 1987). For some of you the practices of learning support may seem a luxury of the past.

Activity 19   From learning support to curriculum development

Now read the rest of Chapter 2 in Reader 2, from section 3 onwards (pp. 44–53). In section 3 the authors describe how they moved on from thinking only in terms of providing support for pupils who experienced difficulties to examining the benefits for the curriculum of having two teachers concerned with planning and teaching joint lessons. They then describe, in section 4, how, through thinking about difficulties in learning as well as about specific curriculum areas, changes were introduced to facilitate the learning of all pupils.

Developing mixed-ability teaching

4.48   At the foundation of the changes at Whitmore is the development of methods for teaching diverse groups. 'Mixed-ability teaching' in secondary schools covers a number of practices. In this school it means the absence of setting by ability as well as the absence of banding or streaming. This is relatively rare in secondary schools but the teachers at Whitmore feel they can provide group or individualized teaching for pupils, in their first two years of school, as is common in primary schools like the Grove. Thereafter, although 'each course in the school is open to all pupils', the nature of the courses involve some degree of guided- and self-selection.

4.49   In their book, Christine Gilbert and Michael Hart produced an 'A to Z of classroom strategies' for assisting the development of mixed-ability teaching in the secondary school:

A to Z of classroom strategies

Arrangements for group work, pair work etc.
The composition of groups can result from friendship, random or teacher-made groups. Their purpose may vary from pupils each performing the same task but working together to situations where each participant has a different contribution to make.

Books and resources at different levels
For example, pupils work from a range of texts rather than one class set of books.

Circus arrangements
Described in the whole-school developments above, pupils may change task when they are ready or in another variation, at set times determined by the teacher.

Drafting

All arrangements whereby pupils have the facility to work through a series of stages before producing a final piece of work that benefits from opportunities to amend previous attempts.

Experiments and empathy tasks

Experiments may be relevant in subjects other than Science, e.g. Geography or Mathematical investigations. Pupils may be the object of an experiment, e.g. if the teacher creates a situation so that pupils experience what it is like to live in a different society or era.

Feedback and audiences

There is motivational value in ensuring that tasks can be seen, read, heard, etc. by other people, including peer groups, family, or the school community. Display work, presentations, videoing, reading each other's work are some possible ways.

Games and simulations

These may be commercially produced or constructed by teachers and can be competitive or co-operative in form. They are applicable in most curriculum areas.

Homework variety

Homework needs to reflect the class diversity as much as classwork. Pupils may complete different amounts in the same time.

Individualized schemes

See Mathematics scheme ... as an example.

Justifying and decision-making tasks

Many activities can involve choices, sorting, selecting, ranking, etc. Pupils contribute actively to the work.

Key facts before extension/reinforcement

All pupils perform the core and then are presented with further tasks depending on their performance at the basic tasks.

Library work and use of resources outside the classroom

Just as the library may present an opportunity to develop study skills, so the local community may provide stimuli and resources not available in the classroom.

Mixed media for pupil response

Writing is not the only way of demonstrating that learning has taken place. Other possibilities include drawing, modelling, tape recording, typing, talking, etc.

Negotiated tasks

Research and other activities result from an exploration of a pupil's interests within overall guidelines and through discussion with the teacher.

Open-ended tasks

The exercise is broadly based so that responses at different levels are possible.

Project work and research with structure

Project work can too often result in the copying of textbooks and little resultant learning. Careful structuring by teacher and pupil can direct the type of material to be sought.

Questionnaires and quizzes

Both tend to be popular because of the active participation needed. The format of quizzes is open to much variation, e.g. pupils might produce the questions.

Role play

This can be used in many subjects other than Drama – History, Science, Geography, Modern Languages.

Supported self-study

In small groups or individually, pupils carry out tasks without constant reference to the teacher, but a group of the class at a time are tutored by the teacher who prepares them for the next task to be completed.

Team teaching

Two teachers work together to plan and present lessons. Both of them would be involved in assessing pupils' work.

Using variety of stimulus resources

Introducing new topics or individual lessons need not depend on teacher talk or textbooks. Tapes, posters, solid objects, video programmes, computer programmes, visits, visitors, pupils' own experiences are some ways of stimulating learning.

Varying basic tasks

Regular activities may be varied. An example is the reading of a set text in English. Apart from the teacher or pupils reading, they can read in groups, take parts, read silently or aloud, make or listen to a tape recording etc.

Working at own rate

Pupils work through a series of activities at their own rate. The topic would be similar for all the class but each could be at a different stage.

(Gilbert and Hart, 1990, pp. 67–70)

NAMING THE ROSE

4.50 In Section 2 I discussed the importance of challenging and avoiding official cliches and jargon about education if we are to think critically about it. Acronyms and jargon seem to hold a particular attraction for workers in special education and sometimes the dropping of one set of terms leads to others which may be more mystifying or may appear to be clumsily euphemistic.

4.51 Teachers who helped pupils overcome difficulties in learning used to be called 'remedial teachers' and their teaching was called 'remedial education'. The terms 'support teachers' and 'learning support' have been introduced in an attempt to dispel the notion that difficulties in learning can be given a quick fix or remedy and to distance the activities of support teachers from the basic skills tuition in 'remedial' classes or in a withdrawal room which was carried out by traditional 'remedial' teachers.

4.52 The teachers at Whitmore wish to signal a further change in emphasis at their school. 'Learning support' may still carry the connotations of remedial teaching as an educational ambulance service, discussed in Unit 6/7, providing the elasticated stocking or truss to keep education on its feet, and may be thought of as providing teaching aides or aids rather than being part of the real business of teaching. The Whitmore teachers now talk of 'learning development' to describe a role concerned with the development of teaching and curricula for all students.

4.53 When people refer to children as 'slow learners' or 'remedial pupils' or 'children with special needs' they may indicate a number of things. The use of such terms suggests a model of education in which children and young people can be divided into efficient and deficient learners. It also hints at exclusionary processes within education, at the operation of a hierarchy of values applied in the school community. But if we stop talking in this way does it mean that all pupils are valued equally and that their needs and interests are thereby satisfied? Or does this merely obscure inequality? What is actually happening is clearly more important than how events are described.

Activity 20 Language matters

Caroline Roaf describes herself as 'special needs co-ordinator' at Peers School in Oxfordshire. She has written about the way 'students' and student groupings are referred to at her school in Chapter 31 of Reader 1. She argues that the terms used to describe students and groupings, success and achievement, reflect and affect the way students are regarded in her school. Read her chapter carefully and consider your reactions to her suggestions. Do you accept that it is important to recognize and avoid the use of racist, sexist or disablist language or other words which devalue students in school? What terms does she suggest that we avoid?

What should we put in their place? Does the use of terms assign differences in value to students? Is the assignment of differences in value a feature of school life that has to be accepted or even welcomed?

4.54 Caroline Roaf's chapter starts with her developing awareness of and acceptance of the need to avoid sexist and racist terms within her school as elsewhere. She accepts, for example, that referring to the active participants in the events of the world as if they are all men and boys can have real negative effects on the way people develop; that talking of skin colour as if it were all rosy pink can imply the invisibility of black students.

4.55 Many people remain unconvinced about the importance of this attention to language and you may be among those who resent being asked to change the habits of a lifetime. Yet the use of discriminatory language is often, simply, rude. One woman headteacher referred to her experience on a panel interviewing six men and three women for a post of deputy head.

> The county's training officer said, 'These are all potential deputy head masters.' He was so insulting. I said, 'Excuse me, there is such a word as headteacher, could you please use it.' He was frightfully apologetic but it runs off the tongue so easily. How insulting it was to sit there as a female headteacher and hear the implication that the only person who could do the job was a man.
>
> (personal communication)

4.56 Caroline Roaf, then, extends the argument to the use of other terms which she asserts 'imply differences in capabilities and worth'. Thus 'low ability', 'more able' and 'mixed ability' are to be avoided unless they refer 'to specific skills or talents'. No student is to be spoken of or thought of or responded to as being generally more able or 'more intelligent' than any other student. She offers a challenge here to pervasive and deep-seated practices in schools and society. This is something that attitudes to ability share with approaches to race and gender. Because racism and sexism pervade society it is argued that schools must have active anti-racist and anti-sexist policies in order to counter them. Do they also need anti-ablist and anti-disablist policies? It has become unfashionable to talk of class divisions in education. Whether this inattention reflects their removal from the structure of society or merely from the consciousness of writers on education will be considered in Unit 11/12.

4.57 At Whitmore, they have based their approach to preventing difficulties in learning on the development of 'mixed-ability teaching'. What does Caroline Roaf offer as a replacement term? Would 'balanced-group' teaching convey the same implications? It seems to lose the ideas that groups differ in attainment and in the way they might learn, though 'mixed-ability' may be a clumsy way of expressing these notions. What about 'heterogeneous group teaching'? The problem with introducing any new phrase is that it's difficult to find anyone who knows what you mean. Would 'mixed-attainment' be more acceptable and informative?

4.58   The course's authors haven't conformed to Caroline Roaf's 'language of mutual respect' by referring consistently to children and young people who attend schools and colleges as students. Perhaps she means this to apply only to secondary pupils. But wouldn't such a difference reinforce status differences between primary and secondary schools and the teachers in them?

4.59   You may find this attention to the language of equality preposterous. You may think that schools should provide healthy competition so that the talents of children and young people can be revealed and applied. Or that it is part of the job of schools to enable students to find a place value in life. But if some students are to be highly valued and others devalued, won't this inevitably lead to difficulties in learning and disaffection?

SUMMARY

4.60   I have covered a multiplicity of issues in this section in varying degrees of detail. Through a case study of the Grove school I have looked at the way present practice in a school can be understood in terms of its history and the background of policy decisions within an LEA. I have examined the way curricula can be shared and differentiated. I have looked at learning support assistants and support teachers and alternatives to policies for centralizing support for children with disabilities. I have considered the difficulties that can arise at transfer to secondary school for children with and without disabilities. Through the case study of Whitmore High School I have introduced the notion of whole-school policies and changing approaches to learning support or learning 'development', from remedial extraction to co-operative teaching to team teaching in mixed-ability groups. Finally I have discussed the language used to describe students, groupings, success and failure in school.

5   INVESTIGATIONS

5.1   All the units in the course will end with a discussion of topics for further investigation. We want you to identify and follow up your own interests and you will have to include one investigation in your assignments. In this unit I have suggested that you begin to identify aspects of education in your own local area that you would like to know more about. Towards the end of the next unit we will consider basic approaches to research, particularly observation and interviewing, which may help you to carry out an investigation. The research we wish to foster through this course starts from an interest in asking a question about something to which you do not yet have an answer.

5.2 In my study of the Grove school I discussed how an examination of one aspect of the education system can lead to an analysis of a wide range of educational concerns. I have started to discuss a considerable number of topics throughout the unit, each one of which could form the basis for several assignment-length studies.

5.3 I have picked out a few possibilities as examples. I have given only a very brief indication of the areas you might look at since the methods you might use to gather information are discussed in the following unit. Any examples we give are there to encourage you to work out an interest for yourself. What you can choose for further local study will depend, among other things, on your job, your family, acquaintances and involvement in education and the use you make of the resources available to you such as the other students on this course. Are you a school governor? Can you join a school trip? Do you know a traveller who would chat to you about their way of life at home and at school? Do you know parents of children or young people with disabilities? Besides using an investigation to find the answer to a question about education that has been puzzling you, you can also use it to check assertions or compare with reports of experiences in the units.

When and why is learning difficult?

5.4 Ask students at varying stages in the education system to identify any difficulties faced in school, now and in the past, for themselves and for their friends. Compare their view of education with your own memories of school and compare these with the perspectives of school workers. Do you or any of your acquaintances work in a school? What makes life difficult for school workers? It might help to try to systematize your enquiries by picking a particular school day and asking your informants to take you through the difficulties encountered.

Care and education

5.5 Can you visit a children's home and discuss perceptions of education with willing members of staff and children and young people? Your local social services department might be able to help you if you contacted them and explained your purpose. You would need to think out carefully what you might want to ask of the workers and children in the home. What do the workers know about the education of the children and young people in their care? What experiences do the young people have of school?

The story of a statement

5.6   Do you know a parent of a child who is the subject of a statement? What has been their experience of the statementing process? Compare their experience with that of Balbinder. Look at the process of compiling the statement, the sense and usefulness of the reports and advice it contains. How do teachers contribute to and regard the process?

A school trip

5.7   What preparation do the pupils have for the trip? What are they expected to gain from it? What presents difficulties for them? How is the content of the trip integrated into lessons at school?

Inclusion and exclusion?

5.8   What is the range of pupils included at a particular school? Who, from the community which surrounds the school, is excluded ? What are the grounds for exclusion?

How and why are students grouped?

5.9   How do the teachers in a primary or secondary school group the students they teach for different activities? What is the rationale behind the grouping? What do students understand about the reasons for groupings and what do they think of them?

APPENDIX 1   WHO'S TO BLAME? A MULTI-LAYERED EPIC

> ... any incident is a climax or crisis in a number of 'stories'. Both pupils and teachers carry their stories with them into school, the clash of stories makes a multi-layered epic.
>
> (Shostak, 1983, p. 113)

1   THE CAST

Mary: The second-in-charge of the school's on-site 'disruptive unit'
Fred: The suspended pupil
Sheila: A history teacher involved in the incident
Carol: The culprit

2 THE SCENE

The summer term is drawing to a close and the atmosphere at Pilgrim's Way is becoming increasingly festive and frenetic. The ritual end-of-year activities – sports days, concerts, day trips, parents' evenings, reports, prize days, fêtes, concerts and plays – are all taking their toll, while teachers struggle to find the extra energy to attend to the final details of next year's timetable, option lists, tutor groups, teaching rooms, planning of new courses, ordering and printing of materials and preparations for the new intake for the coming September. In the midst of it all, of course, teaching is expected to go on as usual.

3 MARY'S STORY

Mary has been working with Fred in the school's disruptive unit for some time and is feeling optimistic about the possibility of his successful reintegration into lessons. However, her day begins not with thoughts of Fred, but with another pupil who has been truanting. She has been asked to call for him at home and bring him into school.

> 8.00 a.m.
>
> Today I have to leave early to collect a school refuser from his home. I hope that this will enable him to settle into coming to school on a more regular basis. However, listening to the weather forecast, it looks like it will mean me getting and staying wet for half an hour longer than usual.
>
> 8.30 a.m.
>
> The steady drizzle turns into rain, and as I arrive at the house I am met by a rather large dog wagging its tail and baring its teeth at the same time. Jack's brother opens the door and the dog goes in, but it is obvious that I'm not going to be let over the doorstep. All manner of strange noises come from within the house, including the sound of Jack trying to fight whoever is using forceful persuasion to get him to come and meet me. Eventually, amidst much cursing from the upstairs of the house, Jack appears and we start the journey to school. Little conversation happens on the way because Jack refuses to talk to me. I can't say I blame him. I feel that I have intruded on his privacy.
>
> 9.00 a.m.
>
> We arrive safely in the unit. I had taken Jack to see his year head before registration period so that they could become reacquainted. This was a partial success. It seemed that the year head was biting her tongue over something that had happened in the past but was desperately trying to appear as if she was pleased to see him. I

didn't witness the whole of the interview because I had to go and remind the head of fourth year about another pupil from the unit who had been out of humanities for two months and is due back to lessons today. On the way back to the year head's office, I bumped into Fred himself and reminded him about going to humanities. He appeared relaxed because they were going to watch a video. His manner confirmed my feeling that he would be all right in lessons from now on. He had made significant progress in managing his own behaviour, or perhaps he had just grown up. When I finally returned to collect Jack, he had a slight smile on his face. The year head looked decidedly grey.

9.15 a.m.

Teaching for the morning under way. Two children are doing maths, one reading, one English, one humanities and two are setting up the computer instead of doing French. I am trying to fill in some admittance details with Jack. After doing this, which takes rather a long time because I keep having to answer questions about which lead goes where on the computer and what a maths problem really means, the first double period has nearly gone and it is time for break.

10.15 a.m.

Break time. Take Jack back into school explaining that he has now got to go back to his lessons for the morning because I am support teaching next lesson, and after that I am teaching my own English group. He gives me a slight smile, only the second time I've seen it today, and makes off towards some friends of his. I go in search of a cup of tea.

10.35 a.m.

Support teaching with a second year group, perhaps the most enjoyable session of the week. I'm supporting this group in lessons because it has three unit pupils in it, and potentially more on the way. It has always struck me that many of the pupils I see in the unit would be better dealt with in their tutor groups and through adaptations to the curriculum presented to them. It can be a very enjoyable experience producing new work for the group and seeing it going down well. And there are always lessons to be learned from seeing it fail miserably! The lesson today is a success. The children work well in their groups and appear engrossed.

1.00 pm

A fairly normal morning. Not so the lunch hour! All interest in my salad roll evaporates when Fred's humanities teacher comes up and tells me she has had a bad time in the lesson with Fred. Apparently, she sent him to the year head for swearing at her. I don't believe Fred could have reacted like this without provocation. It transpires that he was accused of stealing some money by one of the girls in the group and it grew from there. I set off in search of the year head, and after ten minutes spent scouring the building, discover him back in the staffroom telling jokes. He tells me in an off-hand way that the head has decided to suspend Fred for leaving school premises without permission and for using threatening and abusive language to a member of staff. I feel extremely irritated that nobody has bothered to inform me, let alone ask me how the situation should be handled. It is two hours since the head made that decision, but no note or communication from anyone to me. The year head's reaction is that we are all better off without Fred; he's taken up more than his fair share of everyone's time and patience already, and deserves all he gets. He turns back to tell the next joke.

1.45 pm

I catch up with head, who confirms to me that Fred has been suspended because she has had enough of him. I try to point out that several good things have been happening with him as well, but the matter is already closed. The head is more interested in telling me about a meeting next week which appears to mean that there are going to be larger first-year groups next year because of falling rolls, and that we can have no in-service education time for special needs next year because the fourth- and fifth-year curricula have priority. I try to argue that working with an advisory teacher on classroom management will eventually be of benefit to the fourth and fifth years. In return, I receive a speech about who has to carry the can.

1.55 pm

I go back to the staff room feeling very disillusioned with life and find a note in my pigeon hole telling me that Jack did not turn up for his lesson after break. There is no time to do anything about that now. I suppose I will be back on his doorstep tomorrow morning. I leave the staff room thinking that I have one of two choices, getting muddy going back to the unit in the rain or following my pupil's example and going home quietly without telling anyone. I choose the mud only because I'm not as brave as he is.

4 FRED'S STORY

Fred is fourteen years old. He is a fourth-year pupil, and has a long history of difficult, disruptive behaviour stretching back to his primary school days. His teachers have 'tried everything' with him, but apparently to no avail. He seems to have difficulty in grasping what it is about his behaviour that the school finds so objectionable, and feels that he is victimized by teachers because they regard him as a trouble-maker. He looks back on the incident that got him suspended and expresses, with some bitterness, his feelings about it.

My name's Fred and this is my story, although you probably won't believe me. Nobody ever does. I've been at this school for nearly four years now and really, I quite like it. No, not the lessons (I think they're boring), but I like coming to see me mates.

When I was in the first year, they sent me to see a psychologist. I don't think they wanted me at this school, but I said I wanted to stay and he said that I could. Since then things have been all right. I've been kicked out a few times – you know – excluded, but they were for things that weren't my fault. Once you've got a face, you get picked on. Like there was this time when I was fooling around with me mates in the gym. We'd asked to go to the toilet during the maths lesson and the teacher let us. Anyway, we found this tennis ball in the gym which was on the way to the toilet, and we were kicking it around, when it hit the fire alarm and the alarm went off. I got three days out for that. Nobody else did. Something about it being their first offence. It just goes to show that once you've got a face, they'll do you.

I'm supposed to be telling you what happened yesterday. The school has got this unit, and I've been in and out of there for the last few years. It's where they send you when your subject teacher has got fed up with you. I've been in there for science because they said I was dangerous. I ask you! And just recently I've been in there for humanities. I don't know why that was, but it gave me a chance to catch up on me homework and the work in class. Last week, the teacher says to me 'Do you think you are ready to go back to the lesson?' I says 'Yes'. Anyway, they were going to have this video next lesson so I agree to go back. Just before registration, the teacher from the unit saw me and told me to be a good boy and all that stuff. I said I would, 'cause it was the video, see. I went off to register, but I didn't stay in the room because I've got mates all over the school, and it is one of the times of the day that you can see them.

I got to the lesson and everything seemed to be OK. The teacher was in a bit of a huff, but that was because she was late setting up, and there was this girl surrounded by other girls. There was a lot of chattering and the girl in the middle was crying. The teacher went over to them. I suppose she had no choice really, but I bet she thought it was a pain in the neck, first lesson and all that. Then suddenly out of the blue she comes over to me and asks if I was out of my tutor room this morning. I said 'Yes', because I'd been out seeing my mates. Then she tells me in this really snooty voice that some money has gone missing from one of the lockers, £10 to be precise. She asks me again what I was doing out of my tutor room. I've already answered that question, so I guessed she was accusing me of taking it. Well, I'm not having that. I might be a face, but I'm no thief, so I told her where to get off. We had this slanging match, and she told me to get out and go to Mr Hardaway. Fat chance of me going anywhere near him. I decided to go home and let them all cool off.

Anyway, this morning my mum got this letter telling her I'd been suspended until further notice, not because I'd stolen the money – I hadn't, so they can't do me for that – but because I'd used bad language to a teacher. Honestly, who's ever heard of anybody being suspended for swearing when they've been wrongly accused of theft? You ought to hear some of the teachers' language! It goes to show that if you've got a face, they'll do you in the end.

5 SHEILA'S STORY

Sheila is an experienced history teacher. She is also a tutor of a third-year class and takes her pastoral responsibilities seriously, although there is never enough time. Today turns out to be one of these days when the pressure gets too much …

> 8.30 a.m.
>
> There's a cover slip with my name on it lurking by the head's daily notices and I discover that I have won the dubious privilege of an hour's drama with 3L last thing this afternoon in the year base immediately facing the head's office. I'm just getting accustomed to that thrill in prospect, when Lyn, my class's geography teacher, comes beaming into my field of vision. I feel my defences rising. I know when she looks like that it means my class has been playing up again (and somehow there's always a sense that it's a reflection on the tutor when a class is badly behaved). It turns out that she's given the whole class a detention, which she knows is officially against school policy, but she couldn't sort out who the ring leaders were and they drove her to the point where she couldn't think what else to do. She wants to come into my registration period this morning and warn them in front of me to be sure to turn up. (Her confidence in the deterrent effects of my influence is gratifying but, I fear, ill-founded.)
>
> The first pips go as she speaks, and everyone starts pushing past us towards the door. I should be going too, of course, but I can't exactly abandon Lyn in mid-sentence, so I avoid noticing the deputy head in charge of registers who is trying to attract my attention by waving my register in the air. I feel a bit awkward because I want to help but I know that if she comes straight in with me now it will look to my class like I'm taking her side without listening to their point of view. I stall for time to think by asking her to tell me exactly what they were getting up to in her lesson. At the same time, I'm uncomfortably aware of my deputy head's increasingly frenzied gesticulations in my direction.
>
> The scene Lyn describes is all too painfully familiar, but if it was me I couldn't be quite so sure that it was only the kids who were at fault. Still, it's not my place to say so, and anyway if I try to hold

out a moment longer I think the unfortunate deputy head might become locked into permanent spasm. Moving backwards towards the door, I suggest we leave it until tomorrow. She agrees, somewhat reluctantly, and I escape down the corridor. It's a nuisance because I've already got more than enough things to get through in my tutor period today. There's Sukhjit and Helen for one thing. I've been trying to find time to talk to them about homework for days. I suspect that they've got nowhere quiet to work at home, and I might be able to get some arrangement made for them at school. I also intended to get the journals signed up to date this morning. The familiar sense of too much to do and too little time to do it is beginning to build up again. It takes another surge forward as, half-way to my tutor room, I remember I haven't got the video I need for my first lesson. Oh well, I'll have to collect it from the faculty room after registration.

8.50 a.m.

'Late detention for you, Miss!' my kids heckle self-righteously as I scurry towards the tutor room. They pile through the door and I'm grateful that for once they seem prepared to settle down quite calmly. I decide to ignore surreptitious chewing and non-regulation attire for once – much to the annoyance, no doubt, of those who were angling to get sent home to change. There's a limit to what you can tackle constructively at any one time, and I need to keep the atmosphere positive for the discussion to follow.

After the register, I tell them all to bring their chairs into a circle round my desk, and in my best pastoral manner to try to open up a responsible discussion about the problem in geography. The response is predictable, if disappointing. Their faces assume that familiar expression of wide-eyed innocence which they've perfected over years of experience of dealing with such situations. Then they launch into a tirade about how boring the lesson is and how moany the teacher is etc., which is highly embarrassing and exactly what I don't want to happen. I try to steer them off that and get them to consider what they could do themselves to improve the situation, but they just look blank as if they don't see that it's up to them. I find myself saying things like: 'Just because you don't like a lesson, it does not give you the right to be rude or to stop other people from learning', but they don't look any more convinced than I feel. I try not to show it, of course, but underneath I wonder if it isn't more worrying if children *don't* act up when they're bored, but just sit there compliantly and take whatever is meted out to them. I am at a loss to know how to bring the 'discussion' to a constructive conclusion, but the pips solve that for me. I wonder if anything has been achieved by this small foray into pupil participation and democracy. I have my doubts.

Just as they're all bundling off towards the door, glad to escape, no doubt, I remember the notice about lining up for dinners that I'm supposed to have read out to them. I can imagine the chaos (and complaints from colleagues on dinner duty) if my class don't know what the new arrangements are, so I frantically call them all back and make them write the information down in their journals, fending off the groans and complaints as good humouredly as I can manage as the minutes tick relentlessly on. By the time they've finished, the second years due to come into the room have already started arriving outside and are falling over each other trying to press their noses against the glass panel of the door. They think it's a huge joke to hold on to the door handle so that my class can't get out. I issue a few threats and manage to wrench the door open, and then, of course, both lots of children push forward simultaneously so that the sea of bodies presses itself to a standstill. I yell at them to use their common sense, and expend more energy restoring them to some semblance of order before I can make my getaway. I finally head off down the corridor already more than five minutes late for my lesson.

9.12 a.m.

Today being one of those days, my lateness does not, of course, go unobserved. Rounding the final bend, I spy, with sinking spirits, yet another of the ubiquitous senior staff in the process of subduing my fourth year history group outside my teaching room. She looks pointedly at her watch as I scramble up the corridor, still clutching the register which both she and I know should by now have been sent to the general office. I mutter my apologies to her supercilious departing back, remembering I still haven't collected the video that I need to start the lesson.

I'm beginning to feel like I've done a day's work already. The fourth years seem to be pretty 'high', too. Maybe it's only because I'm late. I decide to give us all a chance to calm down, and just mark the names quietly in the register instead of calling them out as I usually do. Fred's back, I see. I wonder if he's the reason for the mood they're in. He always used to have a bad effect on them when he was there before, but he hasn't been in my lessons for a while because he's been going to the unit. I wonder if I should choose him to go down to the faculty room for the video. The others might settle down better without him there, and it might give him a chance to start again on a positive note. I decide not to risk it. He might not feel like doing me any favours yet.

There's a commotion going on in one corner. Sacha is in tears and her friends are fussing round her trying to comfort her. I don't relish the thoughts of sorting out another problem, but no work is going to get done unless I do. I take a deep breath and go over to the group.

Apparently someone has taken her school-journey money from her locker during registration. They say they think it was Fred because he was wandering about the school. I turn to Fred, and before I know what's happening, he starts shouting and swearing at me. The shock of his reaction makes me flip my lid too and before I can stop myself I've told him to get out and report to the year head. As soon as I've said it, I wish I hadn't, because, of course, he just sits there refusing to budge and I've got another problem on my hands about how to make him go short of using physical force (and he's bigger than me, anyway). He stares at me threateningly for what seems like hours, and I'm panicking inside wondering if there's any way I can give in gracefully without losing face with the other children. Just as I'm thinking I'll have to do something, he gets up and slams out of the room with a gesture of defiance in my direction which leaves no one in any doubts as to what he thinks of me.

The relief I feel at his departure is more than compensation, but I'm shaking inside too. It really upsets me to have a confrontation with a kid. Deep down, I'm on their side, but that's not the way they see you. It's so hard to strike the right balance with some of them. If you're nice, they think you're soft. If you're not, they treat you like the enemy. I wish I'd been more careful with Fred, but he just caught me off my guard. I really wasn't accusing him of stealing the money; he just chose to take it that way. And I had to react to him swearing at me. School policy is if they swear at staff, they're out – all the kids know it. I'll go and see the year head at break and explain what happened. Except I'm on duty, so I'll have to settle for a note instead.

The rest of the class are a bit shocked and hushed after Fred's departure. Should I talk to them about the incident or not? I really can't face it, or the video for that matter. I feel completely drained. Better for all of us to escape behind an anonymous worksheet until the pips go to release us.

1.00 pm

I've been so busy for the rest of the morning that I haven't had time to think about Fred again until now. I wonder if the year head got my note. The unit teacher is in the staff room eating her sandwiches and I talk to her about the incident. She hadn't heard about it. In fact, she's very upset and I can quite see why. She's spent a lot of time working with Fred, and now she feels it's all been wasted. She rushes straight off to find the year head, and I feel even worse.

4.00 pm

I've just heard that Fred was suspended because of the incident with me. It turns out that he never reported to the year head (surprise, surprise), but just ran out of school. The head said it was the last straw, that he'd had all the chances it was reasonable to give, not to mention costly one-to-one individual support in the unit. She said you had to draw the line somewhere. I tried to explain that the incident had been partly my fault, but she didn't want to know, nor did the year head. I've got a feeling they're both glad to see the back of him. But I'm left with a terrible sense of guilt.

6 CAROL'S STORY

Carol is fifteen years old and a pupil in Sheila's fourth-year history group. She rarely gets into trouble because she is always one step ahead of everyone else. She appears to have no scruples whatsoever about the money she has stolen, and takes great delight in watching the incident with Fred, enjoying the sense of power she gets from being the one in the know.

> It's been a right laugh in history today. Quite a little *drama*. I could tell Miss was over the top the minute she appeared. Must have got out of bed the wrong side. You'd think that would be a warning to the rest of them to keep their heads down, but not the boys, oh no!
>
> If you ask me, Fred had it coming to him. You'd have thought Fred would have learnt by now that the best thing to do when anyone tries to pin anything on you is to stay cool, look them straight in the eye and deny it. You can be sure I had my excuses ready if anyone happened to inquire how come I'd got ten quid on me when a ten pound note had just done a disappearing trick. But I don't think I'll be needing them now after the way Fred carried on.
>
> You've got to beat teachers at their own game. It's no good looking for trouble, because they'll always get you in the end. You have to pretend to do all the things they want you to do. They love that. Some kids just can't help smirking and shrugging their shoulders when they get told off, to show they don't care. That really gets teachers going. You should watch me and my mate Alison. We can stop just about any teacher in their tracks, no matter what we've done. What you do is: you *smile*, you *apologize*, and you *look as if you mean it*. Magic.
>
> Getting done for swearing is too stupid. Still, it's even more stupid the way these teachers act so touchy when anyone swears, as though it offends their sensitive ears. They must hear people saying the same words every day outside of school and they can't send *them* to the year head. I sometimes wonder how these high-and-mighty teachers manage outside of school, when they can't order people around and give them detentions to make them do what they want.
>
> Anyway, the excitement's over. Fred's gone and Miss looks like she's about to burst into tears. She's handed us this mind-blowingly boring worksheet and told us to get on with it, and now she's sat at her desk with her head in her hands like a silent movie. Well, I'm not about to waste my time doing some stupid questions when she's being paid to teach us. They go on and on about how important our 'education' is, and this is what we get! Out of the window, I can see the second years clodhopping it round the netball pitch, but it's more than my delicate eyes can stand. I nudge my

mate to pass me the magazine she's reading under the desk. She doesn't want to, but she's hoping to get a share in the takings so she can't ignore me. I flip through the pages until the pips go. Some education!

(Mongon *et al.*, 1989, pp. 9–20)

APPENDIX 2 ADVICE ON THE PRODUCTION OF STATEMENTS

Annex 1

ADVICE ON SPECIAL EDUCATIONAL NEEDS: SUGGESTED CHECKLIST

(a) DESCRIPTION OF THE CHILD'S FUNCTIONING

1. Description of the child's strengths and weaknesses

    Physical State and Functioning
    (physical health, developmental function, mobility, hearing, vision and continence)

    Emotional State
    (link between stress, emotions and physical state)

    Cognitive Functioning

    Communication Skills
    (verbal comprehension, expressive language, speech)

    Perceptual and Motor Skills

    Adaptive Skills

    Personal and Social Skills

    Approaches and Attitudes to Learning

    Educational Attainments

    Self-image and Interests

    Behaviour

2. Factors in the child's environment which lessen or contribute to his or her needs

    In the Home and Family, and including the language of the home

    At School

    Elsewhere

3. Relevant aspects of the child's history

    Personal

    Medical

    Educational

(b) AIMS OF PROVISION

1. General areas of development

   (Reference should be made to the relevant attainment targets of the National Curriculum wherever possible.)

   Physical Development
   (eg, to develop self-care skills)

   Motor Development
   (eg, to improve co-ordination of hand and fingers, to achieve hand — eye co-ordination)

   Cognitive Development
   (eg, to develop the ability to classify)

   Language Development
   (eg, to improve expressive language skills)

   Social Development
   (eg, to stimulate social contact with peers)

2. Any specific areas of weaknesses or gaps in skills acquisition which impede the child's progress

   Eg, short-term memory deficits

3. Suggested methods and approaches

   Implications of the Child's Medical Condition
   (eg, advice on the side-effects of medication for epilepsy)

   Teaching and Learning Approaches
   (eg, teaching methods for the blind or deaf, or teaching through other specialised methods)

   Emotional Climate and Social Regime
   (eg, type of regime, size of class or school, need for individual attention)

(c) FACILITIES AND RESOURCES

1. Special Equipment

   (eg. physical aids, auditory aids, visual aids)

2. Specialist Facilities

   (eg, for incontinence, for medical examination, treatment and drug administration)

3. Special Educational Resources

   (eg, specialist equipment for teaching children with physical or sensory disabilities, non-teaching aids)

4. Other Specialist Resources

   (eg, Nursing, Social Work and Welfare Support, Speech, Therapy, Occupational Therapy Physiotherapy, Psychotherapy, Audiology, Orthoptics)

5. Physical Environment

   (eg, access and facilities for non-ambulant pupils, attention to lighting environment, attention to acoustic environment, attention to thermal environment, health care accommodation, privacy of continence care)

6. School Organisation and Attendance

   (eg, day attendance, weekly boarding, termly boarding, relief hostel accommodation)

7. Transport

Annex

STATEMENT OF SPECIAL EDUCATIONAL NEEDS

I — Introduction

1. In accordance with section 7 of the Education Act 1981 and the Education (Special Educational Needs) Regulations 1983, the following statement is made by the .... council ("the education authority") in respect of the child whose name and other particulars are mentioned below.

Child

Surname .... Other names ....

Home address ....

....

.... Sex ....

Date of birth .... Religion ....

Home language ....

Child's parent or guardian

Surname .... Other names ....

Home address .... Relationship to child ....

....

....

Telephone No. ....

---

2. When assessing the child's special educational needs the education authority took into consideration, in accordance with Regulation 8 of the Regulations, the representations, evidence and advice set out in the Appendices to this statement.

II — Special educational needs

(Here set out in accordance with section 7 of the 1981 Act, the child's special educational needs as assessed by the education authority.)

III — Special educational provision

(Here specify, in accordance with Regulation 10(1)(a),

    (a) the special educational provision which the education authority consider appropriate to meet the needs specified in Part II.

(Here specify, in accordance with Section 18 of the Education Reform Act, 1988)

    (b) any modifications to the National Curriculum necessary to meet the child's special educational needs, in terms of programmes of study, attainment targets and assessment and testing

    (c) any exemptions from foundation subjects (specify which)

    (d) details to indicate how it is proposed to replace the exempted programme in order to maintain a broad, balanced curriculum.)

IV — Appropriate school or other arrangements

(Here specify, in accordance with Regulation 10(1)(b), the type of school and any particular school which the education authority consider appropriate for the child or the provision for his or her education, otherwise than at a school, which they consider appropriate.)

V — Additional non-educational provision

(Here specify, in accordance with Regulation 10(1)(c), any such additional provision as is there mentioned or record that there is no such additional provision. Where provision is mentioned, state the providing Authority.)

(Signature of authenticating Officer)

....

A duly authorised officer of the
education authority

(Date)

....

Annex 4

WHAT LEAS NEED TO TELL PARENTS OF CHILDREN WITH SPECIAL EDUCATIONAL NEEDS

1   About the 1981 Act Procedures, and
2   About the 1988 Education Reform Act and its Implications for their Children
3   About complaints under the 1944 Act.

1981 ACT

a. <u>Definitions and Duties</u>

Definitions of special educational needs, learning difficulties, special educational provision.

Procedures for children with SEN.

Duties of LEA to make and review provision for pupils with SEN.

Duties of LEA to provide for children under age 2 and under 5.

Duties of LEA to make integrated placements, subject to the caveats in Section 2(3).

Duties of LEA to make full-time provision up to 19 for all students, whether in school or college.

Duties of LEA under the 1981 Act for young people at school to age 19.

Rights of parents to contribute to assessments and inform discussions.

Rights of parents to have confidentiality.

b. <u>Assessment</u>

Rights of parent to request assessment. Need to prepare parents and to explain proposals to assess. The named officer contact.

Parent's right to a minimum period of 29 days within which to comment on the LEA's proposal to assess the child. Translations of procedures and meetings into other languages.

Duty of parent to submit child for assessment, and parent's right to attend such examinations.

c. <u>Statements</u>

Parent's right to see all the advice on the assessment of the child following a draft statement.

Significance of proposed (or draft) statement and final statements.

Parent's right to a maximum of 15 days within which to make representations to the LEA on the draft statement.

Content of the statement.

Parent's right to receive a copy of the statement.

Consultation procedures.

Identification of any named persons or key workers.

Annual reviews.

13+ reassessments and their significance for the Disabled Persons (Services, Consultation and Representation) Act 1986.

Parent's right to make representations where the LEA propose to amend or cease to maintain a statement.

Procedures for a child with a statement moving into a new LEA area.

d. Appeals Procedure

Explain appeals procedure.

Right of parent to appeal where no statement is made.

Right of parent to appeal against the special educational provision in the statement.

Details of appeals committees.

Details of appeals committees' responsibilities.

Rights of parent to appeal to the Secretary of State.

2. 1988 ACT

National Curriculum

Explanation of: Subjects comprising the national curriculum

Attainment Targets
Programmes of Study
Testing and Assessment

Modifications and/or disapplications to the National Curriculum recorded in the statement and alternative provision being made.

3.   **1944 ACT**

Right of parents to complain to the Secretary of State under Sections 68 or 99 against an LEA which is acting or proposing to act unreasonably or in default of its duties under the Education Acts.

4.   **WHO MIGHT HELP?**

   a.   <u>Statutory Bodies</u>

   LEA services, including the educational psychologist, the remedial teams, support teachers, ancillary workers and any other systems used by the authority.

   Social Services.

   District Health Authority Services.

   Medical/nursing teams in schools.

   Specialist District teams.

   Information Technology Unit for handicapped pupils and students.

   b.   <u>Voluntary Bodies</u>

   National and Local

(DES, 1989a, Annexes 1–4)

APPENDIX 3   THE OPEN-AIR SCHOOL: SUNSHINE, REST AND FOOD

If the Open Air School on the Milton Road at Cambridge is a special school, it is that the children attending there may have a health giving environment – with fresh air, rest and proper food guaranteed. What these children have, all children should have, and the ordinary school functions on the basis that they do have them and concentrates on the things of the mind until physical ills obtrude. The home environment may have been healthy, but the children are deficient, most of them deficient in body, some deficient in mind. Little bodies are strengthened, handicapped intelligences are stimulated.

A SYMBOLIC FENCE

There is a fence at the Open Air School which is symbolic of the rigid division between the two departments. For the backward minds there is a special curriculum, and each child receives more individual attention than is possible in an ordinary primary school, because more guidance is necessary. Psychology is doing its beneficent work. Most of these children are strong in body, and they do not require the special feeding. They have the mid-day meal at the school, but not breakfast and tea. Hand-work has an important place in their instruction, and the school equipment will not be complete until even better provision than at present is made for it. At least that was the impression made on the writer of this article when he visited the school with the Medical Officer of Health. Larger rooms for domestic instruction and for manual training will be required, for in this department the permanent structures have had to be supplemented by temporary buildings. For the children whose minds are struggling towards the light the classes are smaller than on the other side of the school – twenty-five as compared with forty. All teaching is exacting for the teacher, but here patience works miracles among the seventy children who would be handicapped in their own age groups at an ordinary school. There is a feeling of buoyant hopefulness. The work is but beginning, and in that fact alone there is tremendous encouragement. Children are not being left in darkness to struggle unaided, in an environment which is bound to beat them.

PREVENTION

Very different is the problem among the children whose growing bodies need care, and the task of the school is simpler. Minds are bright, but physical strength must not be overtaxed or must be built up. There are

120 and over 96 hangs the cloud of the possibility of tuberculosis. Eighty per cent of them have been sent to the school by the Tuberculosis Officer for the County, Dr Paton Philip, and the headteacher and the Schools Medical Officer work in combination to prevent a favourable field for the growth of the dreaded germ. The Open Air School is fighting to keep the population of Papworth Village Settlement down. It is part of the machinery of the community warring against consumption.

There is a good deal of the atmosphere of the hospital about the school. At its centre is the medical officer's room where the pupils, or the patients – as you like – are examined weekly. The medical history of each is carefully docketed and every increase in weight is noted as something gained, while a fall is a matter for anxious consideration. Personal hygiene is inculcated as of supreme importance, and to realize that it is only necessary to walk into the lavatory, which is something very different to the normal washing place of an ordinary primary school at present. There are the tumbler, tooth brush, hair brush, and comb in a bag for each child, in racks round the walls, and the set of each is a strictly personal thing identified by a number. The washing basins, fitted with hot and cold water taps, in number and cleanliness as such as each school should obtain. There are shower baths in the bath room with the temperature of the water controlled. A trained nurse superintends the cult of the body.

FOOD

The kitchen, too, occupies a commanding place in the school equipment, and the cook and her staff serve three meals a day – breakfast, dinner and tea. The dietary table has a scientific foundation, for it is framed by the Medical Officer, the food is perfectly prepared in a well-equipped kitchen, and it is served in a dining room that encourages appetite. The children are not consulted as to the food placed before them and they eat everything with the complete enjoyment proper to youngsters. The school garden supplies the kitchen with vegetables, and an orchard of young trees is yielding fruit. Milk, butter and eggs are sent direct to the school. Payment of five shillings a week covers the full cost of the food consumed by each child, and when they are able to do so parents contribute that amount. The scale of contribution is based upon a formula, which ensures the cost to the ratepayers is as small as possible. The full contribution is being paid for 75 per cent of the children.

When the children arrive at the school in the morning by omnibus, they divest themselves of their clothing and dress in garments suitable for the season that the sun may do its beneficent work upon their bodies. In the summer time the boys wear cotton slips and they are bare above the waist. The girls have knickers and tunics of cotton. In the cold weather big woollen sweaters are worn. With tanned skins the youngsters do not feel the cold as do their brothers and sisters, whose bodies are not constantly exposed to sun and air.

EPIDEMICS AVOIDED

The midday rest which is imperative in the school is in the open air, and the children are never cold. In wet weather the canvas beds are ranged in open sheds and in winter the children are tucked up in blankets, and each child has his or her own blanket. The classrooms are screened with glass, but the screens are not used without cause, and even when fully screened there is free play for the air above the screens. The result is that epidemics of colds do not sweep through the school, and there has been a 90 per cent attendance in the present year, while the percentage for the whole of last year was 89. In the upper room there was an attendance of 95 per cent.

The period at which a child is at the school varies considerably. Some children are there for a few weeks and return to the ordinary primary school. Others are there for two or three years. It is used as a place of recuperation. All the schools of the future will be open-air schools. The new infant schools planned for Romsey Town and Chesterton will contain many of the ideas of this school, which was designed by the Borough Surveyor after fourteen years of consideration and investigation by the Education Committee. It began in 1914 owing to the public-spirited generosity of Mrs Alan Gray, who placed in the hands of the Committee the means of starting a class at Vinery Road. After the war it was some years before the Town Council could persuade the Board of Education to sanction the expenditure. To get the authorisation required persistent effort, and it was at length obtained when Lord Eustace Percy and the late Sir Geoffrey Butler were together for an hour or two in a railway carriage. The school was opened in May, 1927.

The cost of the school last year was £4,379, from which may be deducted £1,536 for teachers' salaries, and such items as £396 for fuel, light and cleaning. Food cost £982, and the conveyance of children £433. For cod liver oil and malt, the bill was £66. The fees paid for meals amounted to £470.

Everybody in Cambridge knows that the headteacher is Mrs Leah Manning, in the present year the President of the National Union of Teachers, and it ought to be known that she has equipped herself for the post by acquiring a considerable knowledge of methods in open-air schools in Germany and the United States.

(*The Cambridge Chronicle and University Journal*, 8 October 1930, p. 9)

APPENDIX 4   BOB'S STORY

Bob is a teacher from one of the primary schools which feeds into Pilgrim's Way. He is visiting the school today to pass on information about some of the pupils whom he thinks may have difficulty in settling when they arrive in September. Unfortunately, the head of first year will be a new appointment, and so is not yet at the school to receive the information personally.

8.00 a.m.

Today is the day for my yearly visit to the local secondary school about the pupils transferring in September. One and a half hours is all I'm allowed to pass on the information on 50 or so kids! The records we send on are worse than useless really, despite all the time it takes to fill them in. I mean, where is there space to put down the individual things that really make a difference, like 'gets irritable when hungry – needs to be first in to lunch' – and would secondary schools take any notice? What could they do, anyway, about a child who 'can't cope with large numbers of children', or 'can't cope with lots of changes in activities' – that's what secondary schools are all about. So, if you don't fit in, tough!

They're a good lot going up this year, really. My main worry is that I've found out they're going to get a head of first year who's a new appointment from outside the school. Quite apart from the fact that she won't be there today to hear about all the treats in store, how on earth is she going to be able to appear reassuring and welcoming to a new lot of kids when she's feeling tense and strange herself and hardly knows her way around? It's bound to take her time to settle in, and that's just when they need her most. Especially kids like Andy. I just can't imagine him coping at secondary school. He's such a baby still, needs looking after, making special. Who will there be to give him that sort of attention at Pilgrim's Way? Secondary teachers don't expect to have to cosset kids like we do at primary school. Not all of them, of course, but some of them do still need it even in the fourth year, and why not?

8.30 a.m.

I bet secondary teachers don't have to do early morning playground duty either! The playground is already quite busy, and the caretaker informs me that the Robson girls have been there since before eight o'clock. I must tell the head that this is happening more and more often. Andy is standing watching some boys kicking a ball around. He looks miserable, as if he'd love to join in, but doesn't know how to suggest it. He sees me and comes straight over. A ghost of a smile as I greet him. He looks pale and undernourished. He tells me a story about his dog (the same one as yesterday), and then asks to blow the whistle. Who will he talk to when he gets to Pilgrims's Way in the morning? Will he ever get there, after the first few days?

9.00 a.m.

As the kids line up, I notice Vincent towering above them all and remind myself to make a point of mentioning him, too, when I get to Pilgrim's Way. Just his size alone always gets him noticed, and since he's usually around where there's any trouble brewing, he tends to be the first to get blamed for it. He gets resentful because he feels everyone is picking on him, and then he behaves so objectionably that you really do have to pick on him! It could get out of hand at secondary school, where nobody knows him really well. He might feel picked on all the time. Come to think of it, though, just by making a point of picking him out on my visit today, I'm starting the whole process rolling again. You can't win, can you?

9.05 a.m.

Find the head's room to remind him I'm out this morning. He's talking to the school nurse, but beckons me to join them. It's Andy they're discussing. He's lost weight, and they're deciding how to make sure he gets extra helpings at dinner time if he wants them. I ask the head for the list of notes on kids we've compiled together for me to take along today. Some bits and pieces of information are still missing from the record cards, but I am to promise that these will be sent on to them within a week. While I'm there, he asks me if I'd like to go on a course on behaviour problems. I wonder if I should read anything into that?

9.45 a.m.

Managed to get a cup of coffee and the Fun Day Banda sheets run off before I left school. Remembered about Himansu's case conference, but there's not a lot I can do about that because the outcome won't be available until next week, and by then Pilgrim's Way will be completely tied up with their end-of-term activities and certainly won't want any more visits from me. He's another one who will need watching out for, but I can't see him surviving the rough and tumble somehow, no matter how much extra help he gets. But what can you do?

I'm feeling a bit depressed about the whole thing as I pull into Pilgrim's Way car park. The only space is one which says No Parking, so I drive back out and park in the street. I'm just walking back in at the gate, when this large character comes storming past me, virtually knocking me off my feet, makes no attempt to stop and apologize, just goes storming off up the street issuing a torrent of expletives. Am I supposed to do anything? The rate he's going, I'd never catch him anyway. I've got to go to the office to let them know I'm here, so I'll report it to them.

9.50 a.m.

That kid running out made me think of Vincent a few years on, and started me off worrying about him again. The pastoral deputy is not in her office and no one can find her. I'm sitting here waiting, and wondering if it's all just a waste of time.

(Source: Mongon *et al.*, 1989, pp. 20–22.)

REFERENCES

ACKER, S. (1989) *Teachers, Gender and Careers*, London, Falmer Press.

ADES, A., PARKER, S., BERRY, T., HOLLAND, F., DAVISON, C., CUBITT, D., HJELM, M., WILCOX, A., HUDSON, C., BRIGGS, M., TEDDER, R. and PECKAM, C. (1991) 'Prevalence of maternal HIV1 infection in Thames Regions: results from anonymous unlinked neonatal testing', *The Lancet*, **337**(8757), pp. 1562–5.

ADVISORY CENTRE FOR EDUCATION (ACE) (1989) 'ACE Conference: Asian Children and Special Education', *ACE Bulletin*, **28**, pp. 3–4.

ADVISORY CENTRE FOR EDUCATION (ACE) (1990) *Special Education Handbook: the law on children with special needs*, London, ACE (fourth revised edn).

ALLAN, J., BROWN, S., MUNN, P. (1991) *Off the Record: mainstream provision for pupils with non-recorded learning difficulties in primary and secondary schools*, Edinburgh, Scottish Centre for Research in Education.

BAILEY, G. and SKORO, K. (1987) 'Edgewick Community Primary School' in BOOTH, T., POTTS, P. and SWANN, W. (eds) *Preventing Difficulties in Learning*, Oxford, Blackwell.

BINET, A. and SIMON, T. (1914) *Mentally Defective Children*, London, Edward Arnold.

BINNS, D. (1984) *Children's Literature and the Role of the Gypsy*, Manchester, Traveller Education Service.

BINNS, D. (1990) 'History and growth of traveller education', *British Journal of Educational Studies*, **38**(3), pp. 251–8.

BOOTH, T. (1987) 'Introduction' in BOOTH, T. and COULBY, D. (eds) *Producing and Reducing Disaffection*, Milton Keynes, Open University Press/The Open University.

BOOTH, T. and COULBY, D. (eds) (1987) *Producing and Reducing Disaffection*, Milton Keynes, Open University Press/The Open University.

BOOTH, T. and HESKETH, D. (eds) (1987) 'Losing and keeping control: a teacher discussion' in BOOTH, T. and COULBY, D. (eds) *Producing and Reducing Disaffection*, Milton Keynes, Open University Press/The Open University.

BOOTH, T. and STATHAM, J. (1982) 'William: a child with Down's syndrome' in BOOTH, T. and STATHAM, J. (eds) *The Nature of Special Education*, London, Croom Helm/The Open University.

BOOTH, T. and SWANN, W. (eds) (1987) *Including Pupils with Disabilities*, Milton Keynes, Open University Press/The Open University.

BOOTH, T., POTTS, P., and SWANN, W. (eds) (1987) *Preventing Difficulties in Learning*, Oxford, Basil Blackwell/The Open University.

CHIN, J. (1990) 'Current and future dimensions of the HIV/AIDS pandemic in women and children', *The Lancet*, **336**(8708), pp. 134–6.

COMMISSION FOR RACIAL EQUALITY (CRE) (1988) *Learning in Terror*, London, CRE.

CORNWELL, N. (1987) *Statementing and the 1981 Education Act*, Bedford, Cranfield Press.

DE LYON, H. and WIDDOWSON-MIGNIUOLO, F. (1989) *Women Teachers: issues and experiences*, Milton Keynes, Open University Press.

DEPARTMENT OF EDUCATION AND SCIENCE (DES) (1978) *Special Educational Needs*, Report of the Committee of Enquiry into the Education of Handicapped Children and Young People, London, HMSO (the Warnock Report).

DEPARTMENT OF EDUCATION AND SCIENCE (DES) (1985a) *Education for All*, London, HMSO (the Swann Report).

DEPARTMENT OF EDUCATION AND SCIENCE (DES) (1985b) *The Education of Travellers' Children: an HMI discussion paper*, London, HMSO.

DEPARTMENT OF EDUCATION AND SCIENCE (DES) (1989a) *Circular 22/89: Assessments and Statements of Special Educational Needs: procedures within the education, health and social services*, London, HMSO.

DEPARTMENT OF EDUCATION AND SCIENCE (DES) (1989b) *A Survey of Support Services for Special Educational Needs*, London, HMSO (Report by HM Inspectors).

DEPARTMENT OF EDUCATION AND SCIENCE (DES) (1991) *Draft Adddendum to Circular 22/89*, London, HMSO.

DESSENT, T. (1987) *Making the Ordinary School Special*, Lewes, Falmer Press.

DOYLE, C. (1989) *Working with Abused Children*, London, Macmillan.

EGGLESTON, J., DUNN, D., ANJALI, M. and WRIGHT, C. (1985) *The Educational and Vocational Experiences of 15–18-year-old Members of Minority Ethnic Groups*, Stoke-on-Trent, Trentham Books.

EUROPEAN COLLABORATIVE STUDY (1991) 'Children born to women with HIV-1 infection: natural history and risk of transmission', *The Lancet*, **337**(8736), pp. 253–60.

FORDYCE, W. (1987) 'A policy for Grampian' in BOOTH, T., POTTS, P. and SWANN, W. (eds) (1987) *Preventing Difficulties in Learning*, Oxford, Basil Blackwell/The Open University.

GILBERT, C., and HART, M. (1990) *Towards Integration: special needs in an ordinary school*, London, Kogan Page.

GIPPS, C., GROSS, H. and GOLDSTEIN, H. (1987) *Warnock's Eighteen Per Cent*, Lewes, Falmer Press.

GOACHER, B., EVANS, J., WELTON, J. and WEDELL, K. (1988) *Policy and Provision for Special Educational Needs: implementing the 1981 Education Act*, London, Cassell.

GREATER LONDON ASSOCIATION FOR DISABLED PEOPLE (GLAD) (1988) *A Joint Endeavour? The role of parents, parents' groups and voluntary organizations in the assessment procedure for children with special educational needs in three london boroughs*, London, GLAD.

GRUGEON, E. and WOODS, P. (1990) *Educating All*, London, Routledge.

HARDY, T. (1872) *Under the Greenwood Tree*, published in paperback by Macmillan, 1974.

HERBERT, C. (1989) *Talking of Silence: the sexual harassment of schoolgirls*, London, The Falmer Press.

HULL, R. (1985) *The Language Gap*, London, Methuen.

HUNT, N. (1966) *The World of Nigel Hunt*, The Kennedy-Galton Centre for Mental Retardation Research and Diagnosis, Harperbury Hospital.

IVATTS, A. (1975) *Catch 22 Gypsies*, London, Advisory Committee for the Education of Romany and Other Travellers.

JONES, C. (1985) 'Sexual tyranny: male violence in a mixed secondary school', in WEINER, G. (ed.) *Just a Bunch of Girls*, Milton Keynes, Open University Press.

KAHAN, B. (1979) *Growing up in Care*, Oxford, Blackwell.

KAHAN, B. and LEVY, A. (1991) *The Report of the Staffordshire Child Care Inquiry*, Staffordshire County Council.

KENRICK, D. and BAKEWELL, S. (1990) *On the Verge: the gypsies of England*, London, The Runnymede Trust.

LANE, D., and TATTUM, D. (1988) *Bullying in Schools*, Stoke-on-Trent, Trentham.

THE LANCET (1991) Editorial 'Anonymous HIV testing: latest results' *The Lancet*, **337**(8757), pp. 1572–3.

LEE, C. (1990) 'Natural history of HIV and AIDS', *AIDS Care*, **2**(4) pp. 353–7.

LIÉGEOIS, J. P. (1987) *School Provision for Gypsy and Traveller Children*, Luxembourg, Office for Official Publications of the European Communities.

MACDONALD, I., BHARNARI, R., KHAN, L., JOHN, G. (1989) *Murder in the Playground: The report of the Macdonald Inquiry into racism and racial violence in Manchester schools*, London, Longsight Press.

MAHER, P. (ed) (1987) *Child Abuse: the educational perspective*, Oxford, Basil Blackwell.

MALEK, M. with KERSLAKE, A. (1989) *Making an Educational Statement?*, Bath, University of Bath with the Children's Society.

MATTHEWS, H. (1987) 'The place of withdrawal' in BOOTH, T., POTTS, P. and SWANN, W. (eds) *Preventing Difficulties in Learning*, Oxford, Basil Blackwell/The Open University.

MEASOR, L. and WOODS, P. (1984) *Changing Schools; pupils' perspectives on transfer to a comprehensive*, Milton Keynes, Open University Press.

MERCER, J. (1973) *Labelling the Mentally Retarded*, Los Angeles, University of California Press.

MILLER, J. and VAN LOON, B. (1982) *Darwin for Beginners*, London, Writers and Readers.

MONGAN, D., HART, S., ACE, C. and RAWLINGS, A. (1989) *Improving Classroom Behaviour; new directions for teachers and pupils*, London, Cassell.

MORRIS, H. (1925) *Memorandum on Village Colleges*, Cambridge, Cambridge University Press.

NATIONAL CURRICULUM COUNCIL (1989) *Curriculum Guidance 2: A curriculum for all, special needs in the national curriculum*, York, National Curriculum Council.

NATIONAL DEAF CHILDREN'S SOCIETY (NDCS) (1989) *A Mockery of Needs? Parents' experiences of assessment, statementing/recording and appeals under the Education Act 1981 and the Education (Scotland) Act 1981*, London, NDCS.

NAVA, M. (1988) 'Cleveland and the press: outrage and anxiety in the reporting of child sexual abuse', *Feminist Review*, **28**, pp. 103–21.

PYE, J. (1990) *Invisible Children, who are the real losers at school?* (Tony to supply place and publisher)

ROGERS, R. (1989) *HIV and AIDS: what every tutor needs to know*, London, Longman.

ROLAND, E. and MUNTHE, E. (1989) *Bullying, An International Perspective*, London, David Fulton.

SCOTTISH EDUCATION DEPARTMENT (SED) (1978) *The Education of Pupils with Learning Difficulties in Primary and Secondary Schools in Scotland: a progress report by Her Majesty's Inspectorate*, Edinburgh, HMSO.

SEDGEWICK, F. (1988) 'Sort this one out … ', *The Times Educational Supplement*, 28 October 1988.

SHOSTAK, J. (1983) *Maladjusted Schooling: deviance, social control and individuality in secondary schooling*, London, Falmer.

SIMON, B. (1991) *Education and the Social Order 1940–1990*, London, Lawrence and Wishart.

STONE, K. (1987) *The Statementing Process, Professional Power and Parental Interest*, Social Work Monograph No. 51, Norwich, University of East Anglia in Association with *Social Work Today*.

TEW, B. (1987) 'Changes in medical practice towards the child with spina bifida: implications for schools', *Disability, Handicap and Society*, **2**(1), pp. 85–99.

TOMLINSON, S. (1981) *Educational Subnormality: a study in decision making*, London, Routledge and Kegan Paul.

TOMLINSON, S. (1989) 'Asian pupils and special issues', *British Journal of Special Education*, **16**(3), pp. 119–22.

TROYNA, B. (1990) 'Racial harassment in schools', *Highlight* No. 92, London, National Children's Bureau.

WEBB, L. (1967) *Children with Special Needs in the Infants' School*, London, Colin Smythe Ltd.

ACKNOWLEDGEMENTS

Grateful acknowledgement is made to the following sources for permission to reproduce material in these units:

Text

Grove, T. (1990) 'What the Prime Minister said', *The Sunday Telegraph*, reproduced by permission of Mrs Margaret Thatcher; Adams, A. (1990) 'Beaten by a head', *The Guardian*, 19 June 1990; Mongon, D., Hart, S., Ace, C. and Rawlings, A. (1989) *Improving Classroom Behaviour: new directions for teachers and pupils*, Cassell plc; Hull, R. (1985) *The Language Gap*, Methuen & Co; Croall, J. (1991) 'Disability no drawback', *The Times Educational Supplement*, 31 May 1991, Times Supplements Ltd; Sedgwick, F. (1988) 'Sort this one out', *The Times Educational Supplement*, 28 October 1988, Times Supplements Ltd; Gilbert, C and Hart, M. (1990) 'A to Z of classroom strategies', from *Towards Integration*, Kogan Page; *Appendices 1 and 4*: Mongon, D., Hart, S., Ace, C. and Rawlings, A. (1989) *Improving Classroom Behaviour: new directions for teachers and pupils*, Cassell plc; *Appendix 2*: Department of Education and Science (DES) (1989) *Circular 22/89 Assessments and Statements of Special Educational Needs: procedures within the education, health and social services*, reproduced with the permission of the Controller of Her Majesty's Stationery Office.

Illustrations

Page 33: from Miller, J. (1982) *Darwin for Beginners*, Writers and Readers Publishing Cooperative Society Ltd, illustration copyright © 1982 Borin Van Loon, reproduced by permission of Glen Thompson, Airlift; *page 41*: 'Summary of procedures', from *ACE Special Education Handbook*, Advisory Centre for Education (ACE) Ltd; *page 70*: Jacky Chapman.

E242: UNIT TITLES

Unit 1/2 Making Connections
Unit 3/4 Learning from Experience
Unit 5 Right from the Start
Unit 6/7 Classroom Diversity
Unit 8/9 Difference and Distinction
Unit 10 Critical Reading
Unit 11/12 Happy Memories
Unit 13 Further and Higher
Unit 14 Power in the System
Unit 15 Local Authority?
Unit 16 Learning for All